Overwhelmed

OVERWHELMED

Coping with Life's Ups and Downs

by

NANCY K. SCHLOSSBERG

Lexington Books

D.C. Heath and Company – Lexington, Massachusetts – Toronto

Library of Congress Cataloging-in-Publication Data

Schlossberg, Nancy K., 1929–
Overwhelmed : coping with life's ups and downs / by Nancy K.
Schlossberg.
p.   cm.
Bibliography: p.
Includes index.
ISBN 0–669–19543–X (alk. paper)
1. Change (Psychology) 2. Life change events. 3. Change
(Psychology)—Case studies. 4. Life change events—Case studies.
I. Title.
BF637.C4S35   1989
155.9 dc20   89–31459

Published simultaneously in Canada
Printed in the United States of America
International Standard Book Number: 0–669–19543–X
Library of Congress Catalog Card Number: 89–31459

The paper used in this publication meets
the minimum requirements of American National Standard
for Information Sciences—Permanence of Paper
for Printed Library Materials, ANSI Z39.48–1984.

Year and number of this printing:

89 90 91 92 8 7 6 5 4 3 2 1

To my greatest supporter,
STEPHEN I. SCHLOSSBERG

Contents

Part III
TAKING CHARGE

Acknowledgments

W RITING a book is a process that builds on the work of many, with the help of many. My helpers, collaborators, and supporters include:

Editors Ellen Hoffman, Anne Rosenfeld, and Maureen Mylander, who helped me at various times translate my academic ideas into prose; editor Margaret Zusky, who saw this as a book needing to be published; and friend Susan Tolchin, who spent hours helping me write my original proposal and continually urged me to complete this project, even reading an entire draft

Students who tested my work by developing their own studies

Colleagues who supported and encouraged my professional goals; friend and colleague Sue M. Smock, who helped me in the initial conceptualization of the transition model; JoAnn Harris-Bowlsbey and Steve Schlossberg, who read a draft and gave me words of encouragement as well as suggestions

Betty Bowers, secretary and friend, who helps in countless ways, the most important of which is the commitment she shows to my various projects; and Patricia Baker, who patiently typed the early drafts

My friends, who support me as I cope with personal and professional transitions

My husband, Steve, and children, Karen and Mark, with whom I share intimately the joys and sorrows that are part of the adult years

My father, Saul Kamin, who inspired me all my life and inspires me still even though his life has ended

And the many people who have shared their life stories with me, showing their enormous resources to manage change and teaching me that "the best is yet to be."

Introduction

- A woman finds a great job in the city where her lover lives. A year after she relocates she wonders, "Why am I so depressed?"
- After being forced to retire, a man feels his life lacks purpose. Angry at the company and himself, he keeps asking, "Is this all there is?"
- "I am a dumpee," says a woman whose husband of thirty-five years left her for another woman. "I feel like a discarded rag. How will I ever get my life back together?"
- A young man gently cradling his exhausted wife in the delivery room tells her, "He's perfect. He's ours. We're a family at last."
- "How will I construct a life without Al? After fifty years of marriage, he was my life." Even after two years of being widowed, Marge cannot regain her sense of joy and purpose.

Wherever I go, I hear stories of change. All of us face transitions or turning points in our lives. How we handle these journeys, live through them, and learn from them is what this book is about.

Several years ago, my husband and I decided that it was time to leave our home city of Detroit. We planned the move carefully and managed to find jobs in another city where we had friends, colleagues, and children as stabilizing elements. Yet I was depressed for two years after moving.

Why wasn't I weathering this change I had sought? Why was it so hard? This experience prompted me to remember many other changes I had experienced in the past. I found it perplexing that in some instances I had coped successfully and felt like the rock of Gibraltar, while in others I had felt as if I might shatter. As I thought about other people who had experienced transitions like retirement, job change, and family change, I realized that they had also reacted differently, over time, to the same kinds of transitions. I began to search for ways to make sense out of how people cope with life's ups and downs.

I asked my close friend, an expert researcher, whether it was possible to develop a system that would be helpful to people in *any* kind of transition. My friend suggested a way to start: List all the factors that could possibly make a difference in how one copes with change. This list became the basis for my studies of people in transition. With different colleagues, I studied the experiences of people who were going through different types of transitions: men whose jobs had been eliminated, clerical workers who faced job and family changes, adult learners who were returning to school, couples who had moved geographically, and adults who were caring for aging parents.

As a result of these studies—and others designed by scholars studying the adult years—I developed a structured approach that is intended to extend the ways people handle transitions and provide a road map for managing any change.

This is where you come in. Are you thinking about changing jobs, partners, or life-styles? Are you beset by changes you don't expect or want? Have you learned the hard way that times of transition are some of the most difficult in life? Are you excited about the possibility of a new relationship? Are you wondering whether to take early retirement? Do you really believe that adjustment to new conditions, good or bad, can be very difficult? Are you overwhelmed? If the answer is yes, this book can be of special help to you. It provides not just text, not just a theory, but an organized series of activities to help you gain control of your life. That means acquiring a new perspective on transitions, and developing strategies for dealing with them.

Overwhelmed: Coping with Life's Ups and Downs is a self-help book. But it's unlike any you've ever read. It won't tell you how to fix old houses, flabby thighs, shaky bank accounts, or a turbulent love life. It doesn't promise spectacular results in ten minutes or even ten days. What it does do is offer a way to think about some of the most challenging issues you now face and are likely to encounter in the years to come. In a nutshell, it tells you how to cope more effectively with the important changes in your life. I call these changes *transitions.*

Transitions are the changes—good or bad, expected or unexpected—that unsettle our lives, shake us up, and take some adjusting over time. They can be prompted by a host of incidents—a move to a new city, a lost promotion, a new baby, the death of someone close, a financial windfall, an incapacitating accident or illness. These are things that can and do happen to everyone—male or female, rich or poor, young or old, black or white. Yet surprisingly, most people understand very little about transitions or how to manage them creatively.

If someone asked you to run in a marathon tomorrow, you'd probably laugh in disbelief—even if you're a serious jogger. You may be fit, but you're not that fit! A long, grueling race requires special skills and strengths that you don't yet have, that you know can only be acquired through training.

Yet every day people face transitions in their lives that are as taxing psychologically as marathons are physically. And they do this with little or no training or preparation. Small wonder they're often exhausted and overwhelmed. This need not be. I believe that people can become mentally fit, just as they can become physically fit. They can learn to meet the challenge of difficult transitions with grace, skill, and mastery, just as well-trained athletes meet extreme physical challenges.

People train for sports by developing and following a rational plan of action. First they figure out the level of challenge they're trying to meet. Next they size up their particular areas of strength and weakness as they try to work toward that goal. (One person may get easily winded; another's thighs or feet may give out first.) Then they develop a strategy—a personalized training plan—to help in building up their net abilities so they're better organized to meet the challenge and prepare for future demands.

I believe that people can get in shape for transitions by following the same rational principles used in sports training. And I'm convinced that even someone already in the beginning or middle of a transition—someone already running in a race with little or no preparation—can learn to handle it better. That's why I wrote a book about mastering change. In it I present a systematic way of APPROACHING, TAKING STOCK, and TAKING CHARGE of a transition—any transition—so you can master it. The chart at the end of this introduction, "Your Steps in Mastering Change," summarizes these steps. As you will see, the book is organized around these steps:

- Part I, "APPROACHING CHANGE," enables you to look at your particular transition.
- Part II, "TAKING STOCK," details how to assess your resources for coping—what I call you four S's.
- Part III suggests a procedure for "TAKING CHARGE" and profiting from change.

Cases of actual people are used throughout the book to illustrate the system and how you can make it work for any situation—retirement, a major move, any kind of change. You can diagnose your coping resources and assess whether your balance of resources at this time makes the possibility of your changing look good. If there are too many negatives, then you can introduce some strategies to strengthen your coping resources, enabling you to initiate the change at a more appropriate time. If you are weathering change, you can go through the same process—assess your coping resources, see what needs bolstering, and then use your coping strategies to help you weather this difficult time with more options, understanding, and control.

But, you may rightfully ask, what difference can this book make to me? What will I gain by reading it?

First, I have chosen to examine and write about what is common to all adults—the fact that they experience transitions, what those transitions are, and how they change our lives. We cannot predict when someone will marry, divorce, retire, or return to school, but we can say with certainty that all of us will experience and probably require some help in getting through transitions.

Second, having explored the commonalities and the differences in many types of transitions, I offer a method for coping with change systematically. That means all changes. This is not a one-solution recipe for change, but rather a method of arriving at the solution that is appropriate for you.

Third, this book integrates what is known from scholars and researchers into an understandable, practical package without requiring the reader to wade through many pages of technical jargon.

Fourth, this is not an "instead of" book. It is not a substitute for seeking professional help from a counselor, psychologist, social worker, psychiatrist, psychoanalyst, or member of the clergy. I believe that there are situations in which we do need professional help, and reading this book may assist you to decide for yourself if and when it's necessary.

Fifth, the case histories—really stories—generously distributed throughout the book will show you how others handle the problems, challenges, and opportunities associated with change. You may not find a case that is the mirror image of your own, but you can gain confidence and competence as a result of these stories. You will begin to see that there is a structure for dealing with any life change. You will have at hand a system that can galvanize your will and energy for handling change, predict your readiness for change, measure your resources for dealing with changes that have occurred, and offer new strategies to make you more effective and creative in willing and weathering change.

Transitions are part and parcel of adult life. And so is the discomfort they can cause. They can disrupt your capacity to love, work, and play. But transitions needn't be overwhelming. You can master your own transitions by understanding the transition process, recognizing and harnessing your own considerable coping strengths and skills, and selectively adding new ones.

* * * * *

Your Steps in Mastering Change

APPROACHING CHANGE

- Identify your transition:
  What it is
  How it has changed your roles, routines, assumptions, relationships
  The transition process: where you are

TAKING STOCK

- Assess your potential resources for coping with your transition:
  Your four S's—your *Situation, Self, Supports,* and *Strategies*

TAKING CHARGE

- Strengthen your coping resources by selecting appropriate coping strategies
- Develop an action plan
- Profit from change: increase your options, understanding, and control

APPROACHING CHANGE

T HIS section provides basic information about transitions that
will help you initiate the formal process of APPROACHING
CHANGE.

In chapter 1, the dynamics of the transition process are
described, and ways to measure the significance of a particular
transition you may face are suggested.

In chapter 2, you will learn how to identify the many different
types of transitions that surface—predictably or unexpectedly—a
crucial step toward your goal of taking control and profiting from
change.

1

The Transition Process

A N underlying assumption of my approach in this book is that we all face many turning points throughout life. My assumption that a particular change—such as being divorced, becoming a grandparent, or retiring—is not necessarily related to chronological age runs counter to much of the popular literature on adult development that uses metaphors like passages, steps, and seasons.

I believe the metaphor that best describes the adult years is the *fan*. The fan illustrates the growing differences among individuals as they mature. Bernice Neugarten, the psychologist who first brought national attention to the richness and complexities of the adult years, suggests that if you compare a group of six-year-olds with a group of sixty-year-olds, the sixty-year-olds will be the more diverse and heterogeneous. Why? Because with each year and decade, there is a fanning-out process resulting from the many different paths, experiences, and choices people make.[1]

Despite what we know about the adult years, the media often reinforce the metaphors of passages and stages by devoting attention to those persons who jettison their families and jobs for fulfillment as artists, writers, or wanderers in mid-life. But personally and professionally, I am uncomfortable with theories that suggest that a "mid-life crisis" is somehow implanted in the human psyche; those theories give short shrift to the immense variety of other transitions that can affect us at any age.

Less romantic are the data that show that mid-life does not have a corner on the crisis market. In fact, sociologists Leonard Pearlin and Morton Lieberman found that young adults experience more transitions, turning points, and crises in a more concentrated period of time than people of any other age.[2] After all, many in that age group are establishing careers, attempting to form intimate relationships, and moving from their biological families to start families of their own. Yet we seem to read and hear more often about mid-life men and women popping megadoses of tranquilizers in an attempt to cope with the empty nest, returning to the empty nest, or feeling that their time is running out.

If there were one word I could use to describe adults, it would be *variability*. There are grandparents at forty and eighty; first-time parents at twenty and forty; newly divorced people at twenty and sixty. There are new loves and increased sexual activity at forty, sixty, and eighty. There are nearly as many patterns as there are people. In a recent class I asked my students for personal examples of variability. As they eagerly reported their unusual situations, we began to think we could produce an issue of *True Story*. Among the milder stories were the following:

- A student reported that when she was twenty and her mother forty, they had both had new babies. It felt strange to her to have her mother in the same boat as she was.

- A student of thirty reported that her father of fifty-five had married an eighteen-year-old high school graduate. Her attitude toward her father's new wife was very confused; the wife was more like a stepdaughter than a stepmother.

- A student reported that his father had eloped with a woman the same week that his fiancée's daughter (his stepdaughter-to-be) had eloped.

We can probably all agree that though it is tempting to categorize adults, it is not really possible. The differences—the rest of the story—are too great. The fluidity of life, the variability of experiences, and the heterogeneity among adults make it impossible.

It would, of course, be comforting if we could predict the crises or transitions that go along with each year of our lives. But that is impossible. One day at lunch I was talking with a friend whose parents had both died by the time she was thirty-six. She said, ''The death of my second parent created an enormous change for me. It changed the way I saw myself and life.'' Others react similarly when their last parent dies. What is significant here is that the death of a parent sets off a reaction of feelings and needs that emerge regardless of whether the adult ''child'' is twenty or forty or sixty.

But what we know is that each person experiences many transitions, many crises. Let's start our understanding of change with some definitions.

Transitions: A Definition

When we think about transitions in our lives, the ones most likely to come to mind are the noteworthy events that happen to us, expectedly or unexpectedly, like having a baby, being promoted, or losing a job. But some equally important transitions stem from ''nonevents,'' the things we expect and hope for that somehow fail to happen, such as *not* being able to have a baby, or *not* getting a promotion. Both kinds of transitions can bring considerable change. The significance of the event or nonevent lies in how and to what extent it alters our lives.

Here are some clues to search for in determining the significance of a particular transition:

- It can change your *roles*—you have a baby, and suddenly you've become a parent; you change jobs, and you take on a whole new set of responsibilities.
- It can change your *relationships*—being a parent puts you in touch with new people, as does a new job. Both experiences may also transform your existing relationships.
- It can change your *routines*—a new baby alters living and sleeping habits; a new job may require a shift in schedule and in commuting patterns.
- It can also affect your *assumptions* about yourself and the world—a new father discovers he's more protective and respon-

sible than he thought he would be; a person in a new secretarial position may discover personal strengths and weaknesses that went unrecognized in the old clerk-typist job.

If a transition is major, it will change all four aspects of your life: your roles, relationships, routines, and assumptions. If it changes only one or two, it is still a transition, but clearly one of less magnitude.

The same type of transition, such as retirement, can affect people in very different ways. One person may view it as a very positive change—the gateway to a new career or a new life of leisure; another may view it as a very negative one—a one-way ticket to limbo.

Further, what appears to be the same transition may be a major trauma for one person but a minor problem for another. Consider, for example, the lives of two clerical workers, Adrienne and Bette, each of whom was responsible for caring for an aging parent.

For Adrienne, almost everything in her life was altered after her mother—already frail—broke her hip. She had always been dependent on her mother, but now her mother depended on her; Adrienne's role had changed. Her relationships with her own family were changing as well. She had little time for her husband and children since so much of her time was spent caring for her mother. Her routines were clearly changed. Instead of going home after work, she went right to her mother's house, where she spent almost six hours each day until her brother came to relieve her. Only her assumptions about herself were unaltered. She had always considered herself a devoted daughter, and caring for her mother now was consistent with that image.

Bette, also a devoted daughter, was faced with an apparently similar situation, but in her case it was quite different. In Bette's family her sister was the main caretaker. Her mother and sister both felt that Bette should do more, but she had small children and refused to disrupt her own family. So although her role and her routines were not upset nearly as much as Adrienne's were, her assumptions about herself were much more in flux; she felt guilty much of the time.

The outward transition may look the same, but only the person involved can define whether the transition is positive or negative and how it has altered his or her life. Even a positive and not-very-disruptive transition requires a period of adjustment. Transitions that alter life severely clearly demand even more adjustment and possibly more attention. This is especially true if the affected person perceives that transition in terms of extreme hardship.

Today Is Not Forever

Although the onset of a transition may be linked to one identifiable event, transitions take time. Six months, a year, sometimes two years pass before one moves fully through a major transition. Realizing this makes it possible to be kinder to oneself while stumbling through the process and kinder and more understanding to friends who have difficulty coping with change.

Often our first reaction to a transition is extreme, possibly very emotional. Have you ever been jilted? I have. The day of the Big Jilt, I was devastated and thought I would never recover. Within a year, I was happily involved with someone new.

I have interviewed men who lost their jobs because of a plant closing. They, too, felt that they would never recover. One said, "I feel as if I have been hit on the head and kicked in the back. I will never get over it." But six months later he was in a new job and could joke about his earlier desperation. Not all transitions end so clearly or so well, however. Another man in this group who failed to find another job so quickly was still at sea six months after the layoff.[3]

At first you are consumed by the change, preoccupied with thinking and often talking about it. Then there is a middle period of disruption and searching in which old roles and routines change and new ones evolve. This betwixt-and-between period is one of great vulnerability. You're likely to be confused about what to do next, how to behave. Tiny details can become problematic. If, for example, you have just moved in with someone, it takes a while to know where the dishes and glasses are stored. But more important, it takes a while to feel comfortable rearranging them. Finally, when you finish the transition, the change has become integrated into your life, for better or worse. You've accommodated to your new job, city, or relationship.

Time transforms some bad events, but it also alters good ones. One day you marry the person of your dreams or connect with the love of your life and decide to move in together. You think, "I will always feel like this. Nothing will ever come between us." Yet a few months or years later you may have a major blowup and wonder what you ever saw in this person.

In order to illustrate the different ways transitions can change lives, I will relate the stories of three people I know: Carolyn, a newlywed; Cathy, one of the first women appointed to a highly responsible executive position; and myself, moving our family from the home we'd lived in for fifteen years into a condominium apartment. First, the story of Carolyn.

Carolyn the Newlywed

In fairy tales princesses marry princes, ride off into the sunset, and live happily ever after. In real life, even if people do manage to live happily, it can take quite a bit of adjusting to get to "ever after." Carolyn, for example, married her high school sweetheart and moved with him from Cleveland into a small town.

When we interviewed her right after her move, the newlywed said, "If you had a ten-point scale and ten was miserable, I'd be off the scale." Back home she had been part of a tightly knit religious group and had had the support of many close friends and relatives. In her new community she felt isolated. Her husband needed the car to go to work, and lacking convenient transportation, Carolyn stayed in their apartment, without friends or support. To add to her dismay during this lonely period, she had the discomfort and disappointment of a tubular pregnancy.

In an interview six months later, Carolyn sounded very different. She had worked to overcome her isolation and was making some headway. After negotiating the use of the car, she joined a religious group similar to the one at home and even started a newcomers' club. She had also arranged regular phone chats with family and friends in her old community. "I'd still rather be back home," she said, but she no longer felt like a complete outsider and was beginning to build a new circle of friends.

Carolyn's story shows us that when you reflect on how you felt at the beginning of a transition and compare it with your feelings about it later, it's evident that a transition does not happen only at one given point in time. Rather, it is a process—an episode with a beginning, a middle, and usually an end. And all through the transition, your reactions and emotions continue to change as you integrate the event or nonevent into your life.

Cathy the Executive

Consider the example of Cathy, who was recently promoted to a top executive position—one of the first women to fill this role. At first, the newspaper articles about her thrilled Cathy and her family; she could think of nothing else. But now that she has been in the job for three weeks, she is beginning to feel very confused. The excitement is over, and she is not sure how to behave, how to feel. Cathy is particularly bothered by her new role supervising her former colleagues; she feels isolated from them. The very people she's normally leaned on for support are now the ones she's supposed to lead, evaluate, and even fire if need be. This is her betwixt-and-between period, one that can last from a week to several years. If she adjusts well, she will become used to her new role and its power and even come to enjoy it. If she does not, she will suffer, lose confidence, become depressed, and perhaps seek another, less stressful job.

Whether the transition turns out for better or worse, it is still a slow process during which roles, relationships, routines, and assumptions keep changing.

The Moving Family

My own story relates to my husband's and my decision to invest our entire savings in purchasing an elegant new apartment. But once I had moved in, I found myself feeling miserable and guilty. This appeared to be an elected, highly desirable transition, but in fact the move triggered tears instead of smiles.

Our house needed extensive repairs, and our son was a senior in high school preparing to go to college. With a minimal amount of soul-searching, my husband and I decided to sell our home. Thrilled when we were quickly offered the asking price, we moved to an apartment building that allowed dogs, and we proceeded to invest in extensive redesign and decoration.

Before moving in, we had three worries: Would we fit into the space? Would the renovations be finished so we could move in? Would our son adjust? We felt we could handle anything. After all, we had elected this transition, and we were copers.

The complaints started the day we moved into the apartment. Our dog, the construction, and our teenage son all became subjects of a neighbor's gripes to the manager. Even though the "best" dog trainer in the city pronounced our dog normal and the neighbors in need of training, I still felt guilty and anxious every time I left the dog alone in the apartment. Petty accusations increased— our guests rang the wrong doorbell; our son walked through the lobby without a shirt. I felt I had been suddenly transformed from a desirable neighbor into a pariah. I did not want to move back to a big house, but I wondered if I could ever learn to tolerate the "condominium mentality."

As time went on, I began to enjoy the condo and all its resources, but even then it seemed that every time I relaxed, something else went wrong. I was amazed by the amount of adjustment this elected transition required. One day I was in tears about the move and my husband, Steve, said, "You're the expert on transitions, so get out your model." I thought, "The system is for other people. It can't work for me!" Then I realized that if I was going to stand behind it, I had to apply it to myself. I assessed my *Situation, Self, Supports,* and *Strategies* and then looked to see whether

I could either change these, change their meaning, reduce the pressures, or do nothing. Here's what I came up with.

I realized I could change the *Situation* if I wanted to. If life got unbearable, we could move back to another house. I also reminded myself that today is not forever and that my reactions would change over time.

Second, I looked at my external resources, especially *Supports,* and realized that although my general supports were good, a negative support system was operating in the apartment. I decided to find at least two people with whom I could develop a good relationship. As I walked my dog and swam in the pool, I finally met two women who were delighted to have us as neighbors. Next I analyzed my inner strengths, my *Self.* The most important thing, I realized, was to stop blaming myself and start thinking differently about the *Situation.* Once I convinced myself that the neighbors weren't right after all, then my guilt reaction was replaced by assertiveness. When the next complaint came, I wrote back and said, "I refuse the complaint. Furthermore, I have a complaint to make—I feel we are being harassed."

Postscript: This process started with excitement about the move. We then went through shock about the complaints, soul-searching about whether we had made the right decision, and—finally—contentment with the move. Now I am delighted to live where we do. Our son has moved to his own apartment nearby, and I no longer care about complaints from neighbors.

Many who write about the transition process suggest that people go through sequentially specific stages from beginning to end. In fact, they give labels to each stage. My research and experience lead me to conclude that life is not that orderly. The labels don't work. What I have found is the following: If the transition is major (if it has altered your roles, routines, assumptions, and relationships), you will be consumed with it at the beginning, as we were. Then you will experience a middle period, during which you will learn the ropes but still feel betwixt and between. Eventually you will incorporate the transition into your life, as we did. I rarely think about the move now, although on occasion I miss the informal atmosphere of a house. On balance I have concluded that the benefits of my new home outweigh the losses, and I hope I have learned that today is not forever. Reactions to good and bad transitions change over time, and an important factor in APPROACHING CHANGE is recognizing that we need time to adjust to them.

APPROACHING CHANGE:
A Perspective

There are a number of assumptions embedded in this approach. One is that transitions can be either positive or negative, but if they have altered your life in significant ways, you will need to cope. The more your life is altered, the more you will have to bring your coping resources to bear on the change. Even if members of a group appear to be in the same boat—as we saw with the job loss group—each has unique problems that require unique solutions.

This approach to life's transitions differs from the popular tests or scales that assign a given number of ''stress points'' to various transitions. Those tests assume that stress is inherent in the transition. In my system, however, I assume that what may appear to be the same transition will alter different people's lives differently. My system helps you to identify and analyze both your own characteristics and those of the transition, and to assess how much the transition has altered your roles, routines, relationships, and assumptions.

APPROACHING CHANGE requires knowing what change is, how you appraise it, and how much it has altered your life. The next chapter describes the multiple types of change you will encounter—an important aspect of APPROACHING CHANGE.

2

Transitions:
Their Infinite Variety

T o help in understanding transitions, we'll look next at their
infinite variety. Some are exciting, wonderful changes we
never expected. Others we dream about for many years before
finally taking the plunge and making them happen. Still others are
sad losses that—expectedly or unexpectedly—alter our world.
Since all of us dream of doing things that will change our lives,
let's start this section with a discussion of elected transitions: the
ones we choose.

Elected Transitions

Many of the transitions in our lives are ones we initiate. We have
been brought up to expect—and elect—certain ones because they
are major events in the lives of most people in our society. These
transitions are social milestones, such as graduating from high
school, moving away from home, getting your first real job,
marrying, having a baby, retiring. Not everyone chooses to experience all these transitions, but many people do, and there is strong
social pressure to do so.

As transitions go, social milestones are somewhat cushioned
for us in a number of ways. Because these events are expected,
we usually have a long time to think about them and to plan and
rehearse for them. And there is usually an abundant supply of
role models to show and tell us how to handle them. In addition,

as we enter these transitions, we often get a helping hand from members of our community who celebrate our change in status with us.

Other changes involve those that we initiate. These are individual choices that are outside the social timetable and are therefore more idiosyncratic. Some of these choices, such as shifting jobs or moving, are commonplace; they are generally socially condoned, as long as we don't hop around so often that we seem inordinately restless or unstable. Other individual choices, such as separating from a spouse, moving back into your parents' home, or changing religious affiliations, may even run counter to the prevailing social norms. Nevertheless, we sometimes choose such changes when it looks as if they may somehow improve our lives or at least make them less difficult.

However important or positive such transitions may be for us, there's usually little social ritual or celebration for most of them. They are largely private choices, typically shared with only close family and intimate friends.

Let's look more closely at examples of these two types of chosen changes: social milestones and individual choices.

Social Milestones

The fact that we've been raised to expect to go through certain transitions in our lives, can prepare for them, and are likely to have social support and approval when we choose them doesn't necessarily make them easy. And the fact that these transitions are common doesn't mean that everyone experiences them in the same ways. A few examples should make this very clear.

High School Graduation. Jane has just graduated from high school. Graduation was an expected transition, and her school and family helped her make plans to go to college after graduation. But she did not feel ready to grow up. In fact, she stopped studying during her final semester, ending with a grade point average below C. The admissions counselor at the only college that had accepted her called to say they needed to rethink her admission; she wouldn't be allowed to start in the fall. Jane is betwixt and between. She has left high school, but does not really know what is next.

Most of her friends handled this transition quite differently. They graduated with reasonably good grades, found summer jobs to help pay for tuition, and despite some trepidation are looking forward to entering college in the fall. For them, high school graduation is an exciting opportunity to take the next step in life. But for Jane it is a threat; she resents being pressured to grow up and move out of her family's home.

Retirement. When we compared interviews with newly retired people and recent high school graduates, we found that, despite the many different issues facing each group, both had a strong sense of being betwixt and between.

The retired group we interviewed consisted of partners and their wives from a large company that required retirement at age sixty, despite new legislation eliminating age as a factor in retirement policies. During the two days we spent with them, it was clear that they were now facing what they knew was inevitable: giving up an immensely important part of the life they had known and valued for many years.

We discussed how this expected transition was likely to change their lives. As one wife said, "I don't think Don realizes how important his relationships at work have been. What will he substitute for them?"

One former partner who had retired two years earlier reported his surprise and dismay when he returned to the firm to have lunch with an active partner and realized that the partner viewed the occasion as a duty. For the retired partner, the biggest shift was the transition from being needed—indeed, central to the success of the company—to being marginal, even an annoyance. He hadn't yet found a new place to anchor his identity.

Another former partner felt quite different about his retirement. He had recently remarried and was thrilled at having much more time to spend with his new wife, getting to know her family, and fashioning a new life with her.

Thus a social milestone, whether it is high school graduation, retirement, or any other major expected event, is intrinsically neither good nor bad. It marks the end of one episode of life and the beginning of another. For those who focus on what is ending, it can be a threatening change. For those who focus on it as a beginning, it is an opportunity to explore and conquer new worlds.

Individual Choices

Paul Gauguin abandoned his career as a Parisian stockbroker to devote himself to being a painter in the idyllic setting of Tahiti. As he once wrote to his friend, Swedish playwright August Strindberg, "You suffer from your civilization. My barbarism is to me a renewal of my youth."

Why does Gauguin's story have such appeal? Maybe it touches our secret dreams of starting out fresh. Almost all of us respond in some way to news stories of men and women who shed their lovers and their jobs to take off in an entirely new direction.

Few people actually abandon all their ties to the past. But at certain points in life many people do choose new jobs, new communities, or new lovers. Let's consider a few examples of the kinds of individual choices people make.

Terry—From Editor to Entrepreneur. One day Terry, an editor in a publishing house, sent a letter to one of his clients, who was writing a book on mid-life. "Dear Jean," he wrote, "I have enjoyed working with you on the book. As you know, I think it is a real winner. In fact, it is so good that I have taken it to heart and am writing to tell you that I have resigned from the company; I am leaving publishing and am opening a boutique in Carmel. As I was working on your manuscript, I kept thinking, 'What about my life? Is this really how I want to spend it? Isn't there more to life than editing other people's manuscripts?' As you can see, I decided to give it a try and change gears. Thank you for inspiring me to take the leap, and good luck to you."

Lisa—To Atlanta with Love. I don't know how things turned out for Terry, but I do know something about my friend Lisa, who also shifted gears but in a different way. Recently relocated from Omaha to Atlanta, Georgia, Lisa had moved for several reasons. In general, she was ready for a change, but she also wanted to be geographically closer to her lover of many years; she had also found a good job there. In her new city she had a ready-made support system of friends, a house to move into, and a high-prestige job. Nonetheless, when we had lunch about a year after her move, Lisa said she felt very confused and depressed. Since her relationship with her lover and her job were both working out pretty well, she couldn't understand why she felt this way.

Lisa didn't realize that although the change she initiated was a positive one, it still required many adjustments: daily life with her lover, a challenging new job, an unfamiliar city. She had been part of another world with set relationships, roles, routines, and assumptions. Now all these were changed. She hadn't foreseen how long and confusing the betwixt-and-between period would be, or how long it would take to learn the new "rules" and figure out where she fit in.

We often think these kinds of confusion and discomfort happen only in response to negative changes. But any major transition, even the one we dream about and freely choose, is a process of adjustment. This process includes an awkward period in which our old roles, routines, and assumptions are no longer valid while the new ones are not yet in place.

Surprise Transitions—
When the Unexpected Happens

Although many of the transitions in our lives are ones we initiate, there are many we can never anticipate. In brief, they're surprises, both good and bad. Your closest friend is in a serious car accident. You're fired. You make a killing in the stock market. You're passed over for a key promotion. A major film studio buys the rights to your first novel.

If the unexpected happens, you're in for a surprise—and possibly a transition. Whether the surprise is terrible or delightful, it can tax you emotionally and challenge your coping skills. Here are a few examples:

Dolores the Rejected

After thirty-five years of marriage, Dolores's husband announced that he felt too young to "dry up"; he had fallen in love and was leaving to join the new woman in his life. What really stunned Dolores was that her husband had fallen in love with a woman his own age. She couldn't even rationalize his behavior as one of those mid-life May-December flings. "It completely knocked me off my pins," she said. After two years of depression, she decided to return to school, where she is now getting a nursing degree. She is still angry and somewhat depressed, but as she puts it, "At least I'm working on something."

Bill's Second Chance

Bill, too, had been depressed for several years, but for a different reason. His thirty-year marriage was going strong, but he was very unhappy in his work life. He had taken early retirement from a high-level position in the United Nations—a job that required a great deal of political know-how and made him feel useful and important. Knowing he was not ready to quit working, he had joined a small consulting practice where his focus shifted from "saving the world" to "getting clients." He hated worrying about every "billable breath," but he felt that at age sixty-four, this was the best he could do. He would come home at about 4:30 every day, putter, and watch TV. Bill told his wife he felt like a "has-been." Several friends suggested therapy, but he resisted. He was a classical example of a man caught in an unsuccessful transition.

One day, out of the blue, Bill was offered a top position that enabled him to return to public service. He accepted it on the spot and left the consulting firm. The new job, he says, is "just what the doctor ordered." He has been rejuvenated. Although he now works twelve-hour days and is on a grueling travel schedule, he says, "I am the luckiest man in the world—at sixty-four to be given the chance to do an important job." He had taken a risk, but he was ready for it. "God willing, I plan to spend another ten years at it," he says.

Bill's story is unusual in several respects. First, a totally un-expected opportunity made the real difference. Instead of spending the rest of his life in low gear, he is on the road, growing and con-tributing. Second, since he had never adjusted well to his consult-ing job, the shift back to a more familiar and congenial type of work was liberating, not disturbing. True, his routines are dis-rupted by lots of travel, but his assumptions about himself are unchanged and indeed reinforced by his new job: he is a man who loves public service and who also has had the good fortune to find a second rewarding career.

Nonevents: When the Expected Doesn't Happen

We can be just as surprised when expected events don't happen as we are when unexpected ones do happen. The expected ones that fail to materialize—called *nonevents*—can pack just as powerful a wallop in our lives.

One researcher, Janice Chiappone, has analyzed how the non-event of infertility affects couples who want and expect to have children.[1] When they finally realize that pregnancy will not occur, this nonevent kicks off a transition. The researcher found that the impact of infertility is much greater on the women than on the men. But once the women accept the fact that they cannot have children, they begin to make different assumptions about their relationships and roles—especially their work roles. For example, one woman in the study had been coasting along on a series of low-level temporary jobs. But when medical tests confirmed that she could not become pregnant, she began to make plans to return to school and become a speech therapist.

Harry, the Chief Who Never Was

Nonevents in our lives are often more difficult to handle than events are. They are usually not public; others can't see them, and unlike many expected events—especially social milestones—there are rarely any rituals to help us cope with them. For example, the realization that one will never be promoted to a coveted position at work can alter a person's self-image and expectations for the future. Yet one does not announce this transition to the world or mark it with a ritual. Here's how one person reacted to this nonevent.

Harry had been waiting for years for a promotion to bureau chief at his newspaper. "At first," he says, "when I did not get my promotion, I thought it was because I was so young. As the years passed, I began to wonder: When? Finally, at age forty-five, I came across an article that explained that many organizations stop promoting people after they turn forty, and I suddenly realized that the answer to my question was: Never! It was upsetting to realize that some people defined me as too old, even though I felt no different from what I was like in the past. I was not getting something I had always wanted. I blamed myself, and I blamed the system."

After wrestling for many months with his anger and frustration, Harry started to look for a new job, but he found nothing better than the one he already had. He then set his sights on a new goal: early retirement. Although he continued to perform his duties well, he stopped being a workaholic and started to see himself as "putting in time." Instead of working late and taking work home on weekends, he started using his free time to explore investment opportunities and new career paths that he might follow later.

Harry's nonpromotion was a classic nonevent and very painful at the time. But some nonevents, like the one described below, are like a gift from heaven.

Melissa's Gift of Life

Melissa was an active, vibrant woman who worked as a free-lance writer. Her work, though emotionally and financially rewarding, was isolating and hard. When she learned she had a rare and fatal illness and had little time left to live, she gave up her career and decided to spend her last months being close to her children, bravely preparing to die. But to everyone's surprise and delight, Melissa's illness remitted, and she lived. Strangely, even this almost miraculous turnabout was a transition and required adjustment. But she joyfully embraced the nonevent and returned to her work as a writer. This time, though, she was less compulsive about work and built in more family time.

Life on Hold:
The Transition Waiting to Happen

There's a special type of situation that I call "life on hold." It's a transition waiting to happen, poised between an event and a nonevent but really neither. For a variety of reasons, usually beyond your control, you can't bring about the change you want, but you haven't given up on it either. A few examples will show you what I mean.

Ted on Hold

Ted had always dreamed of being a journalist. After graduating from college, he landed a job as an editorial assistant at a national magazine. But he soon discovered that he had become a glorified clerk-typist, and the job was a bore. Although he was encouraged to write in his "spare" time and the magazine printed a number of his short articles, Ted still felt that he was wasting his time doing other people's "dog work" and that his plan to work his way up the organizational ladder was not panning out. Staff turnover at the magazine was rare, and he feared it would take forever to get a real writing position there. Ted was raring to leave.

When an exciting new magazine advertised for writers, Ted applied immediately and got exactly the job he had wanted. He was to start in a month. But during that month he started having strange physical symptoms and began a round of medical tests. No one could quite figure out what was wrong. Some doctors suggested it was "nerves," and others suggested a number of dire possibilities. He started some treatments, but they only made him feel worse. By the time he was to start the new job, he was embroiled in medical tests with undefinitive results and lacked the energy to take on the challenge of the new venture.

Suddenly it wasn't so clear that he should leave the old job for the new one. Ted knew that he was valued in his old job and that he would have the support of his boss and office friends even if he took a lot of sick leave. He also had health insurance coverage for his mounting medical bills, but it wouldn't start at the new job until he had passed a three-month probationary period.

It was a heartbreaking decision, but he turned down the new job and put his career growth on hold. He decided to stay temporarily in his outgrown position and concentrate on finding someone who could diagnose and treat his puzzling disorder.

The Saga of Slow Shep

Vicky, like Ted, was working in her first job after college graduation. She had found a "dream" position in a prestigious design studio and had taken it even though it meant she'd be three hundred miles away from Shep, her lover, who was completing his graduate work. Since Shep had often talked about finding a job in her city after he got his degree, Vicky initially expected that they'd be separated only a year, until he graduated.

To overcome the strain of separation, Vicky and Shep called and wrote to each other regularly and maintained a commuting romance. Many of their weekends together were spent at the weddings of friends, who kidded them that they were "next." They both felt a growing sense of commitment to one another and at times talked about marriage, although they weren't engaged.

But then one year stretched to two, and although their relationship was clearly deepening, she began to worry that it might never lead to a long-term commitment. When his dissertation was almost completed, Shep announced that he was starting to look for jobs in other cities as well as in hers. Vicky began to get angry. She felt it was time for them to live together and test their relationship under conditions more normal than weekend trysts. Shep said he felt the same way but that he didn't want to confine his job search to one city. When Vicky hinted that she'd give up her job and relocate if that was the only way they could be together, he said he couldn't ask her to do that, and it might not even be necessary if things worked out right.

Vicky feels caught in a bind. She sensed that they are entering a crucial stage in their relationship, one that could well end in marriage. Yet she is not sure that Shep is ready for the next step. She needs him to commit himself to living with her wherever he winds up working.

Vicky's life is on hold. She feels too committed to Shep to date other people, but she cannot wait for him indefinitely, and she doesn't want to resort to "tricks" to make him join her. She has decided to "back off" from the issue of commitment and the crucial issue of the "next step." There's a major transition in sight, but it's not clear yet whether it's a breakup or an engagement.

Sleeper Transitions

Many transitions have an identifiable beginning point, such as a wedding, a move, or the death of a loved one. When they start, we're well aware that change is under way. But some transitions called *sleepers* start much more subtly and just creep up on us over time. It may be a gradual process of packing on pounds or slipping deeper and deeper into drinking, smoking, or using drugs. Maybe it's a matter of ignoring a worsening health problem, or a pattern of increasingly slacking off at work, or spending more and more time away from the family.

We don't consciously choose to do these things, but they can and often do change our lives eventually just as if we had. At some point we realize that there's been a big change for the worse. We have arrived at the point where our roles, relationships, and routines have all been altered. Yet in this case, our assumptions have failed to keep pace.

A similar but more constructive kind of sleeper transition can bring us—equally unaware—to a new place in our lives. Perhaps you've been growing and developing on the job, becoming more skilled and confident. You may be finding work increasingly unchallenging and boring but haven't given any thought to other career opportunities. Or perhaps you've become more worldly, interested in new foods, books, ideas, or friends, while your part-

ner is stuck in a narrow sphere of interests and aspirations. Many
people find it hard to imagine that over the years they have grown
apart from someone they love.

At times, constructive and destructive sleeper transitions happen
together. Frustration with a relationship or a job we have unwit-
tingly outgrown may contribute to avoidance or to sliding into
harmful habits as a way of coping. Being utterly absorbed in an
avocation we love may lead us to ignore many other commitments,
obligations, and relationships—even our health.

Sleeper transitions of both types are tricky because we are usually in the midst of them before we recognize them. Even if you're
growing, if you don't recognize the changes taking place and
they're leaving you out of sync with your existing world, you can
be in a very precarious position. By the time you realize how much
you've changed, your behavior may already have kicked off a
chain of events that precipitates an unexpected major transition.
Here's the story of Dan, a friend who told me about his experience
of waking up just in time to take advantage of a sleeper.

Sleeper Dan

He was a much-valued technician in a biology laboratory, a man
whose "magic" solutions for thorny technical problems had
earned him the nickname "Dr. Fix-It." He enjoyed his work and
his excellent reputation, but over the years Dan found himself
increasingly absorbed in his weekend avocation, handcrafting
stained glass. He had started by making little window hangings
and had progressed to more ambitious and time-consuming projects such as elaborate decorations for Victorian doorways. He
entered a few craft shows, sold a few pieces, and started to receive
commissions, first from friends and then from strangers who had
seen and admired his craftsmanship.

Dan found himself designing projects and sketching whenever
he had a spare moment—even at his regular job. But one day a bad
evaluation by his supervisor made Dan realize that his heart was
no longer in the lab, but in his home studio. With a wife and young
son to support, Dan had never considered his stained-glass proj-

ects as more than a hobby. But the shock of the poor job evaluation made him look more carefully at how his time and energy were invested, and he realized that he would like to devote all his energy to working with the stained glass. To his surprise, when he shared his dreams with his wife, Bev, she was very supportive.

After taking a business course for artists and craftsmen, he saw that with careful planning, hard work, and a little luck, he might be able to shift careers and still make ends meet—barely. Together, Dan and Bev developed their ''five-year plan'': He would set up a formal business and try to establish himself as a professional craftsman while continuing in the lab. Bev would serve as his business manager and publicist. In a year or two, if the business seemed to be taking hold, he'd try to shift to doing the stained-glass work on a part-time basis, and a few years later, he would finally work on the stained glass full time. Once their son was a little older, Bev would return to work to help finance the business.

With this plan and goal in mind, Dan was able to keep his two work worlds separate. He went to his job in the lab with new energy and enthusiasm, and his work improved.

Double Whammies:
It Never Rains but It Pours

Although the case examples I've given on the preceding pages are drawn from real life, you may have noticed something unreal about them: For the most part, they sound as if people deal with a single transition at a time—even a single type of transition. But we all know it never seems to happen that way really. Events and nonevents never seem to come in single file. You might elect a transition, look forward to it—and then all of a sudden things begin to fall apart all around you. You're going to have a baby, and then your husband tells you he has just lost his job. You just moved in with a lover, and you discover that your mother, in failing health, wants to move in with you. Events in one area of your life trickle or tumble into other areas, and each one makes managing the others somewhat more difficult.

At times it feels as if the stars must be out of joint; surprises spring up, all unconnected, but all disruptive. At other times the transitions are part of a chain reaction in which one transition sets off a host of others. I call these pileups of related or unrelated transitions *double whammies.*

Sometimes one event sets off a chain reaction, and your life feels like one crisis after another. Trouble erupts at every turn, for you and for everyone around you. Fortunately, for most people, these situations are fairly rare. Tough as they are to weather, most people manage to get through them. As the old saying goes, "When the going gets tough, the tough get going."

It doesn't take a string of catastrophes to add up to an overload of transitions. Even a run of good but disruptive transitions can bring on Excedrin headaches and more. Here are a few examples of the way some transitions can pile up at difficult times in our lives.

Unretiring Ben

The story of Ben, a man in his sixties, makes it clear that transitions often come in sets and can ricochet in unexpected directions. Ben began, well in advance, to make plans for his mandatory retirement from his company. He had no control over its timing, but because it was expected, he had time to prepare for it. He returned to graduate school to study accounting. As he says, "My strategy was to get into something new and leave the old completely behind. I resolved not to be a hang-around, not to keep going back to the old outfit."

Although older than many of the other students, Ben made friends easily and even started a support group for incoming students to the program. At first he was excited about preparing for a second career, but the school transition unexpectedly triggered some upsetting family transitions.

His wife, Ava, became increasingly critical of the fact that Ben was a student and no longer producing income. Somehow this unleashed mutual hostility that had been pent up for years. They decided to separate; but to maximize their financial situation, they lived separate lives in the same house until Ben received his degree and got a job. Later, Ben and Ava divorced, and not long afterward he remarried.

The multiple transitions in Ben's life seemed to start with just one—retirement. That prompted a return to school, followed by marital problems, eventually followed by a new job, a divorce, and remarriage. Ben's story illustrates the reality that transitions rarely happen singly. Rather, one elected transition can lead to an unexpected one, and then a whole train of other transitions may follow.

Mary—Caught in the Middle

Mary is a middle-aged graduate student whose recent life is a study in transitions. Before she had a chance to grieve for the deaths of both her parents, her aged in-laws decided it was time to move to a nursing home. Because her husband, the breadwinner, couldn't afford to take leave from his job, she commuted out of town regularly to help his parents plan their move. At the same time, Mary's daughter, unable to afford her own apartment, moved back home; and her son and daughter-in-law had a baby just as he lost his job. To an outsider, Mary's situation was obviously overloaded with transitions. Yet she was so unaware of the cumulative impact of these changes in her life that she could not understand why it was so hard to complete her graduate degree!

Because our lives are often intertwined with other people's, our own lives may change when people close to us undergo major transitions. Mary's life had become a perfect example of what sociologist Gunhild Hagestad calls "countertransitions"[2]: everything that happened to her was the result of other people's transitions.

The Nature of Transitions

Transition events and nonevents that change our lives come in many sizes, types, and combinations. But it is not the actual event or nonevent that is most critical, but understanding how—and how much—these changes alter our lives, and what we can do about coping with them. In part II we will look at ways to analyze transitions more effectively and to understand the personal attitudes and characteristics that we bring to them.

* * * * *

Types of Transitions: A Summary

Elected: Some are social milestones; others are individual choices

- Graduating from school
- Moving away from home
- Changing jobs
- Having a baby
- Retiring
- Moving
- Divorcing
- Becoming a grandparent

Surprises: When the unexpected happens

- Car accident
- Winning the lottery
- Death of a child
- Plant closing
- Getting a raise

Nonevents: When the expected doesn't happen

- Infertility
- The promotion that doesn't occur
- The book that is never published

- The fatal illness that disappears
- The child who never leaves home

Life on Hold: The transition waiting to happen

- The long engagement
- Waiting to die
- Hoping to become pregnant
- Waiting for Mr. or Ms. Right

Sleeper Transitions: You don't know when they started

- Becoming fat or thin
- Falling in love
- Becoming bored at work

Double Whammies: It never rains but it pours

- Retiring and losing a spouse
- Marrying, becoming a stepparent, and being promoted to a first supervisory job
- Having a baby, developing a serious illness, getting a new job
- Caring for ill children and parents at the same time

And many others

TAKING STOCK

S OME of us breeze through what others may find a tragedy. Some feel panicked and lost even when their dream—a move to a new house, marriage to the perfect mate, landing the job they've always wanted—is suddenly coming true.

Because each of us has a different personality and because every transition has its own special meaning for each, there's no simple slogan or formula for coping that can be used universally.

The next three chapters will offer some guidelines on how you can assess any transition that confronts you. By TAKING STOCK of the four S's, as outlined in these chapters, you will build a foundation of understanding—both of the nature of transitions and of your own reactions to them—that is essential to achieving the goal of mastering change.

In chapter 3 you'll learn how to take stock of your *Situation;* in chapter 4, of your *Self* and *Supports*—your inner resources and the friends, family, and other individuals and institutions on whom you can rely for help; and in chapter 5, of your *Strategies*—what skills you have or can learn that can help you cope more effectively.

3

TAKING STOCK
of Your *Situation*

ALL of us **APPROACH CHANGE** with potential resources for managing change—what I call the four S's:

- your overall *Situation*
- your *Self*
- your *Supports*
- your *Strategies* for coping

By taking readings on the state of these resources, you can assess how well equipped you are to deal with the transition in question. For example, most people move a number of times in their lives. Sometimes they cope well; other times they manage only with great difficulty. The reason: their *Situation, Self, Supports,* and coping *Strategies* differ with each move. TAKING STOCK of these four S's will give you a reading of your potential resources for managing change.

This chapter will guide you in assessing one of your four S's—your *Situation.* When you think back on all the transitions that you have made in your lifetime, you can probably remember some that you handled rather well and others that you handled less smoothly and with less satisfactory results. Since you are the same person, it may be puzzling that you could have pulled through one change like a trooper and yet floundered in the face of other, apparently less severe changes.

In chapter 2, I described different types of transition events and nonevents, showing that some are anticipated and planned for, while others are unexpected and catch us by surprise. Some alter our lives dramatically; others do not. To understand your own *Situation,* it helps to identify your transition and try to attach one of those labels to it. But in order to take some of the mystique out of your transition, I suggest going beyond the label and asking yourself a series of questions:

- How do you evaluate the transition?
- How has the transition, irrespective of type, changed your life—now and in the future?
- What are some of the characteristics of your particular transition in terms of your planning for it, its timing in your life, your control of it, your previous experience with similar transitions, its permanence, and the presence of other stresses in your life?

Your answers to these questions will differ with each of your transitions. Some transitions you will evaluate as negative, others as positive, and many as a mixture. Some transitions will change your life in every regard; others in more limited ways. And some you will be able to plan for and control, but others will seem overwhelming and out of your control. Some will occur at a bad time in your life and add a burden to the stresses you already have, while others will add zest and sparkle to your life.

In this chapter we will review a list of factors that you must assess, consciously or unconsciously, when you TAKE STOCK of your *Situation:*

- your evaluation of the transition
- how the transition has changed your life—its impact
- the transition's characteristics

Your Evaluation of the Transition

Individuals appraise similar situations in different ways. As demonstrated by the truism about a glass of water, some of us are innately more optimistic than others: an optimist is likely to see the glass as half full, while the pessimist will describe it as half empty. The metaphor can be applied to the way you view life in general. But although one tendency may dominate, most people swerve in and out of optimism depending on the situation.

Though a particular kind of change may seem only negative, it is impossible to make assumptions about how people will react to it. In our study of job loss, most subjects saw the change very negatively; however, one nurseryman reported that he didn't care about losing his job because he felt sure he could get a job someplace else. Another person who saw opportunity rather than disaster was a top executive. "This is great," he said. "I am so bored with my job, my wife, my life. This gives me the excuse I needed. I'm leaving everything and moving across country."

A famous line from Shakespeare's *Hamlet* is illuminating: "There is nothing either good or bad, but thinking makes it so." In other words, to one person a serious illness can be the devastating last straw that destroys hope. But to another, it can present a challenge to take control and beat the illness down.

Some researchers have addressed this idea that how people view transitions affects their ability to cope with them. In a study of college students, for example, several psychologists found that the students' assessment of their own competence to handle exams was a better predictor of achievement than grade point average or SAT scores.[1]

One participant in a study about women's friendships reported that she was distraught about a rift that she felt was killing a thirty-five-year-old friendship. By talking through the situation with her therapist and reading books on women's friendships, she began to see that she was in the midst of a shifting relationship, not a final rift. She reevaluated her *Situation* from negative to okay. This modification enabled her to cope with the changing relationship.

Psychologist Richard Lazarus contends that individuals are constantly asking the question, "Is it good, bad or neutral?" not just about the transition itself but also about their own resources for coping with it—what I call their four S's.[2] Throughout life our resources change, prompting us to reevaluate our *Situation*.

This book will show you how to shift the balance of your resources when they are needed to cope effectively. When that occurs, your evaluation of your transition can change.

The bottom line is this: Your evaluation of a transition is the most critical aspect of how you handle it. You are more likely to embrace the change if you see it as one for the better or simply as neutral than if you see it as negative.

How the Transition Has Changed Your Life

We must be cautious about judging the severity of an event simply by labeling it. A transition that is severe for one person may be relatively minor for another, depending on the degree to which it alters the person's roles, relationships, routines, and assumptions.

Change in Roles and Relationships

All of us enact many roles in life. We are friends, parents, children, co-workers, employees, employers, neighbors, students, teachers, and much more, depending on the circumstances. And in each of these roles, we have particular relationships with our family and others around us.

As I discussed in chapter 1, some transitions are minor and alter these roles and relationships insignificantly, while others are major and alter them in major ways.

Examples of transitions that can change our roles and relationships significantly include divorce, having a child or a grandchild, seeing our children grow up and leave home, moving into a better job or losing a job, graduating from college, or undertaking a new career in middle age. A divorce means that we lose a partnership and the role of spouse, and it can also mean that we lose neighbors and sometimes friends. The same is true when we lose a job. When we change jobs and are required to make a move, we lose neighbors and friends and perhaps group membership, but we gain a new role in the work force.

In analyzing a transition, it is useful to delineate the role changes. Which are gains and which are losses? Even if we gain new roles in the course of a change, the more roles that are altered, the more we have to adapt. We must remember that with role changes come changes in routines, in relationships, and in assumptions.

Changes in Routine

Some of us do not realize the importance of routines in our daily life until they are changed or eliminated. Even minor routines—taking a coffee break with a co-worker who is a valued friend or watching the news every night at seven o'clock—provide us with an important measure of serenity, solace, and comfort.

In one case, a widow and mother of three children married a man with three children of his own. She expected difficult role changes, especially when the whole family moved into her house. She acquired not only a husband and a larger family but the role of stepparent, which brought with it a changed relationship with her former in-laws and a new relationship with her new in-laws. She had expected to undergo some difficulty with her role changes, but the additional difficulties of adjusting to new daily routines came as a surprise. All the logistical and mechanical issues of daily life—who makes the beds, who washes the dishes, who drives the carpool, who shops and cooks—suddenly had to be renegotiated. In another case, a woman and her children moved in with her new husband and his children. As the husband said, "The forks and knives were no longer in their 'right place.'" It took a while to get used to all the changes.

Some people regard changes in routine as positive. For example, one writer who moved from New York City to France basked in her change of routine. She says, "I found it easier to change *almost* everything at once—where I lived, what I ate, how I exercised, my work routine—when I went to France. Sometimes I have felt jarred when my routines change, but because I was seeking change, this time it was exhilarating." This writer's experience underscores the point that the *amount* of role or routine change is not the primary factor in how we weather a transition. It is how we evaluate it.

Changes in Your Definition of Yourself

I often lead workshops on transition. In these, I ask the participants what changes are the most difficult. The answer is often the same: events that change one's definitions of oneself are the most difficult to endure. One participant recognized that her problem is common to many women. She held an important job, but she was frightened by the responsibility. It took about one year for her to realize that she could not only do the job but do it well. She began to define herself as someone who is comfortable with being in control. In another, less happy case, a man who lost his job and could not find another began to see himself as worthless and therefore unemployable.

Transition Characteristics

As you evaluate your transition, you will define it in terms of whether you can plan for it and its timing in your life, the degree to which you can control it, whether it is fleeting or permanent, and how it fits into the rest of your life.

Your Ability to Plan

If you can anticipate a change, you can rehearse for it mentally, and often that makes the change easier. One woman rehearsed her departure from her husband for three years. She knew exactly what she was going to do on the day that she left, so that when the time came, the inevitably painful transition was somewhat less anguishing.

My colleagues and I are just beginning a study of men and women executives as they leave their jobs.[3] We are learning that one major difference in people's ability to cope is the degree to which the leaving is voluntary and planned. Leave-taking is often difficult, but when you can plan for it and rehearse for it, it is easier. It is this notion that has prompted many companies and organizations to start preretirement planning programs.

Timing

The timing of a change is often as critical to your reaction as the type of change. Does the event come at a particularly difficult time in your life? Two men recovering from open heart surgery may have very different reactions to the operation and different levels of optimism about recuperation. One, for example, may be in physical pain, but he may believe he is facing a bright future with a loving partner and a secure job. The other may have been abandoned by his wife, or his child may have been diagnosed with a severe illness, or he could be jobless. He will find it harder to dream of a better day.

Other examples with built-in timing problems include events such as a family move during the summer before a child's senior year of high school; a company layoff just before the employee's pension rights are vested; and the diagnosis of a serious illness in one partner of a couple about to marry. These unfortunately timed changes can double their normal impact, making it far more difficult for an individual to go through a change. Of course, a change can also occur when it is expected, or at an unexpected but ideal moment, making it much easier to cope. One forty-five-year-old woman wanted to move to New York to work for many years. But she feared that because of her age and her relatively provincial background, no one would hire her. But with perfect timing, she was offered a fantastic job in New York just as her youngest child was going to college. In spite of her nerve-wracking adjustments to combine a serious career change and a dramatic move, she was able to face these more easily with her nest empty.

In analyzing a transition, it is also important to consider another kind of timing: the timing within the transition process itself.

As discussed in chapter 1, each transition is like a journey, with a beginning, a middle, and an end. At the beginning you think constantly of the change. The middle period is one of disruption, when you find yourself at sea: old norms and relationships are letting go, and new ones are not yet in place. In the final period, you begin to fit the transition into the pattern of your life.

Control of the Transition

Transitions that are forced on us are far more difficult to manage than those we make by choice. In our study of men whose jobs were eliminated, one theme emerged: they were as concerned about their lack of *control* over the job loss as over the actual loss itself. One man told me that he felt the experience had been the most difficult in his life.[4]

Family members may be affected in very different ways by a change in the job status of one person in the family. One psychiatrist has written about the trauma experienced by women who are asked to follow their successful husbands around the country as the husbands changed jobs.[5] Such moves for a promotion demand very different coping strengths in a family. The spouse who is being promoted has elected the change and is often excited and happy about the move. The spouse who follows feels forced into it by the need to keep the family together. This "follower" often feels depressed and unsettled, leaving friends, routine, and a familiar home. Children in such a family have different responses, depending on their *Situation, Support, Self,* and *Strategies.* Grandparents may feel very sad about "losing" an entire family. If invited to join the move, they might feel powerless. If not invited, they might feel deserted. We can, however, generalize, that the more you feel you can control a situation, the more likely you'll be able to manage it and to reduce the toll it takes on you.

Previous Experience

Drawing on your previous experience of similar transitions can help you get through the one that's facing you now. The trick is to turn what you learned before into a positive experience, rather than a negative one.

It is true that previous experience can determine what follows. Consider the example of two people who are facing surgery. On the basis of previous experience, one patient may be able to focus on the anticipated surgery, rehearse for it, and prepare by recalling the factors that gave him or her control and comfort during past surgeries. Another patient may feel terrified because of previous negative experiences. For this patient, the key might be to identify what made the previous experience negative—a dislike for a particular hospital or doctor, for instance—and try to determine how those factors can be avoided or ameliorated the second time.

Similarly, some families in the armed services or the foreign service say that they get used to resettling and even thrive on the experience by viewing the move in terms of the challenge of meeting new friends and becoming part of a new culture and life-style. Yet for other families the stress of such moves can add up until finally someone says, "I've had it. Never again."

Previous experience is an important factor in coping, but only the individual involved can determine whether it is a plus or minus.

The Permanence of the Transition

We regard a permanent change differently from one that we think of as temporary. It is easier to endure even very painful transits if we know that they won't last too long. For example, although no one looks forward to surgery, a brief stay in the hospital for a minor operation is easier to cope with than a diagnosis of a lifelong disability. A man may agree to move to another city so that his wife can enroll in a two-year training program, but only on condition that the move is temporary. He may need to be reassured that they will return to their home community when her training is completed.

On the other hand, it feels good when something that is going well is seen as permanent. When interviewed by a television correspondent on *60 Minutes,* the new head of Disney Productions said he loved his life at that moment—his family, his job, his money—and he wished that it could last forever.

The Rest of Your Life

None of us leads a static life. Our lives are changing constantly, and the same transition may influence you differently under different circumstances. The other stresses in your life influence how you handle a particular transition. Consider the story of Julia, a clerical worker. She underwent a major transition in her life—her husband's loss of his job. When she described this event to me, it became clear that she and her family were already deluged with stress. Her daughter Joan had been living with heart disease. Joan was president of her school class and an active skier and tennis player, and the family had to believe that the teenager's case was exceptional, that she would recover. Yet at almost the same time that her father lost his job, Joan suffered a serious relapse and was hospitalized. This forced the family to face the prognosis that the youngster's life really was at stake. Earlier that year Julia's father had undergone eye surgery, and her mother-in-law had died recently. "I feel like a multiple-problem family," said Julia. The family felt stretched to its limits. Any one of these transitions—all undeniably negative and unchosen—could reduce one's ability to cope. Bunched together, this set of changes all but incapacitated this family.

Some changes—even elected changes—can be disruptive. For many people, coping with lots of changes at once can cause stress. Whether you evaluate lots of change as stressful or not, it does require an ability to choose from and sometimes to use lots of strategies. To understand how an individual approaches and responds to a particular transition, it is necessary to look at the range of factors that add up to the context of the person's entire life.

Summarizing Your *Situation*

As you think about making a change or weathering an existing one, you can ask yourself a series of questions about your *Situation*, your *Self* or inner strengths, your *Supports*, and your coping *Strategies*. In this chapter we have focused on your *Situation*.

Is this *Situation* good or bad from your point of view? Is it positive or negative? Is it expected or unexpected? Does the transition come at the worst possible time or the best? Is it a move up or a move down? Where are you in the transition process—at the beginning, the middle, or the end?

When confronted with a transition, especially an unexpected or undesired one, it is easy to view your *Situation* as irrevocable or permanent. Yet as we have seen in this chapter, analyzing a transition systematically shows that each one is different, that some are more significant than others, and that any irrevocability may be more deeply rooted in our own psychological makeup than in reality.

You can improve your ability to cope with transitions by learning how to measure the impact of a particular change: by placing it on a continuum of time and seriousness; by examining the effects it has had on your roles, routines, and relationships; and by becoming more aware of the effect of your own personality on how you view the situation.

Before going on to look at two other crucial S's—your *Self* and your *Supports*—you can review this approach to analyzing your *Situation* by filling out the chart entitled "Your *Situation* Review."

* * * * *

Your *Situation* Review

Did the situation change your

Roles	Yes No
Relationships	Yes No
Routines	Yes No
Assumptions	Yes No

Were you able to

Plan for the transition in advance	Yes No
Control the transition	Yes No
Benefit from previous experience	Yes No
Was it a good time in your life	Yes No
Were there many other stresses in your life	Yes No

Did you evaluate your situation as	Yes	No
Positive	Yes	No
Negative	Yes	No
Okay	Yes	No
Taking everything into account, do you feel your situation is		
A high resource	Yes	No
A low resource	Yes	No
A mixed bag	Yes	No
Okay	Yes	No

4

TAKING STOCK of Your *Self* and Your *Supports*

I N the last chapter we learned how to take stock of the *Situation* surrounding a transition. This chapter will help you take stock of two more crucial factors—your inner strength or your *Self* and the *Supports* that surround you.

When you complete this chapter and the next one (which will help you identify your potential coping *Strategies*), you will have gained more knowledge of your own resources for coping, of the areas in which you are weak, and of some ways you can shore them up.

Your *Self*

We all bring many personal resources to our transitions. Some of these, like financial assets, are tangible. Others, like personality or outlook, are less obvious but just as important.

What do you bring of your *Self* to the many transitions you face? When you try to answer that question, you get into the interesting but challenging task of defining who you are. We have all heard people say, "You would really like Jane. She has a wonderful personality." What does that mean? Does it mean that Jane has traits that are considered "good" in our culture or group? Does it mean that Jane handles life with ease? Does it mean that she has a way of looking at things that make her a pleasure to be with? These questions show that the process of understanding ourselves and what we bring to a transition is a complex one. Yet we all know that a person's behavior and outlook are very critical to managing change.

Different Ways to Look at Steve

The case of Steve, the president of a medium-size organization, may help us understand different ways of assessing what inner strengths we can bring to managing change.

Steve had a good income, good health, and many friends; he was married to his college sweetheart. He felt "on top of the world." But that world shattered when Steve and his vice president had a falling out over the direction the company should take. The rift became so serious that the board decided that one of them had to leave. After a long political struggle, Steve was asked to resign. He felt crushed. At fifty-eight, he felt too old to go looking for another job. Soon after, his wife died of a heart attack. Steve had to face two transitions so potentially devastating that each alone would have exaggerated his fears of aging and loneliness.

After several years of struggling, Steve is now working at a new job he created in a social service agency. He has met new people and has developed some very close relationships. Many of Steve's friends attribute his eventual triumph over two difficult transitions to his inner strengths and resources. Since we cannot touch or see someone's inner resources, let us examine Steve's case to help us understand how we can actually TAKE STOCK of our inner resources. In doing so we can draw on the work of a number of psychologists and researchers who have devoted their careers to this problem.

Some would say that Steve has a "hardy personality" that enables him to TAKE STOCK and TAKE CHARGE of his life. Others would point to his resilience and flexibility, which are invaluable in enabling someone to bounce back and change course. Others would point to Steve's wisdom, perspective, and humor—all strengths that can be significant in dealing with life. The question hotly debated in the field of adult development is whether these characteristics are inborn, genetic, or learned. I purposely am not entering that debate in this book. But regardless of whether these are innate or learned qualities, it is my conviction that all of us can increase our coping strategies, thereby becoming more flexible and resilient. As we will see in chapter 5, the person who uses many strategies flexibly is the one who masters change. I believe we can learn how to increase our coping repertoire and build on what we already have.

A "fighting spirit" is another label that might be applied to Steve by a psychologist who has studied women with breast cancer.[1] In the study she identified five types of people according to how they responded to the illness. A follow-up study showed that the "fighting-spirits"—those with the will to fight, struggle, and resist—and the "deniers"—those who refused to recognize the reality of the situation—had less recurrence of the disease. The other three types—the "stoics," who submitted without complaint to unavoidable life circumstances; the "helpless persons," who felt unable to cope without the help of others; and the "magical thinkers," who believed that help would come through mysterious and unexplained powers—all had higher recurrence rates.

Another way to take stock of your *Self* and your inner resources is by identifying the degree to which you feel good about yourself—what Grace Baruch, Rosalind Barnett, and Caryl Rivers have called a sense of "well-being." In their study of three hundred women, they tried to determine the factors contributing to well-being. Some of the women they studied had never married, others were married without children, some were married with children, and others were divorced with children. The authors found that those who put energy into several areas of their lives, such as work and family, were more satisfied than those who put all their eggs into only one basket, such as work or family. The ability to invest in several aspects of life results in a "sense of mastery," a feeling of being "important and worthwhile, and . . . finding life enjoyable."[2] The authors concluded that the combination of mastery and pleasure is what generates a sense of well-being.

In the case of Steve, we can assume that he was overwhelmed

at first because his sense of well-being had been totally disrupted. His balance of mastery and pleasure was shaken. But because of who he is, Steve was able to take on this challenge and once again gain control and balance in his personal and work life.

When you are in transition, you often feel helpless. A partner leaves you, your plant closes, birthdays keep accumulating, you choose to move to a new city. Many people experience these events as overwhelming. Are you the kind of person who usually gives up? Or do you meet the challenge head-on and try to take control?

Psychologist Martin Seligman's work has focused on different ways people react, especially to negative, uncontrollable, or bad events. According to Seligman, those who feel they have control over their lives, or who feel optimistic about their own power to control at least some portions of their lives, tend to experience less depression and achieve more at school or work; they are even in better health. Seligman suggests that the individual's "explanatory style"—the way a person thinks about the event or transition—can explain how some people weather transitions without becoming depressed or giving up. Since many transitions are neither "bad" nor "good" but a mixture, a person's "explanatory style" becomes the critical key to coping. A person with a positive explanatory style is an optimist, while one with a negative style is basically a pessimist.[3]

For example, we can ask how Steve explained what happened to him. Did he blame himself and say he lost out on the job because he was inadequate? Did he conclude that he would always be inadequate at work? People who blame themselves for everything that happens and then generalize to think they always "screw things up" have a good chance of being depressed and passive. On the other hand, Steve saw that he clearly had some role in the job decision and that, in general, he handles complex situations well; he thus had a good chance of coming out on top in a transitional situation.

Steve's success in managing and weathering his transition suggests that he is probably an optimist and that his "explanatory style" is positive.

Seligman and a colleague also suggest that a person's explanatory style can predict his or her success on a job. In a study of insurance salespersons, those representatives with a "positive explanatory style" were twice as likely as those with a "negative style" to be still on the job after a year. Following up on this study, a special force of a hundred representatives who had failed the insurance industry test but who had a "positive explanatory style" were hired. They were much more successful than the pessimists.[4]

Another way to TAKE STOCK of personal resources is to use personality tests such as the Myers-Briggs Type Indicator. This test, developed by Isabel Myers and Kathryn Briggs, is based on Jung's descriptions of different "personality types." This easy-to-score, easy-to-take personality test gives someone an indication of how he or she habitually views life and its problems and makes decisions about how to handle them.[5]

Some of us navigate through life by using intuition, and others navigate by using senses, like eyes and ears, to uncover the facts in a realistic way. Some people make decisions in a logical, systematic way; others do so by feeling what seems right. People can be differentiated along these dimensions. It may be helpful for you to try to determine how you and your family or acquaintance tend to function based on these criteria. Recognizing that your type might be different from that of your partner, boss, or friend may help you understand, for example, why you work well with one colleague and conflict with another. It could be a simple matter of different ways of understanding and approaching the world. Acknowledging these differences can be helpful in building collaboration rather than conflict.

I have used words like *stress, transition,* and *coping.* These words are used by psychologists in many different ways. Some define *stress* as an outside stimulus; others define it as a response to a stimulus. Others, like Richard Lazarus, define *stress* as a "particular relationship between the person and the environment that is appraised by the person as taxing or exceeding his or her resources and endangering his or her well-being."[6] Others who face major transitions—those that change many roles, routines, relationships and assumptions—as Steve did may be challenged by them. According to Lowenthal and Chiriboga, Steve, who faced a very stressful set of transitions, was nevertheless challenged rather than overwhelmed. It is the interaction of the *Situation* and the *Self* that explains reactions to transition.[7]

To summarize: To TAKE STOCK of your *Self* and your inner resources, you can ask yourself some questions:

- Are you generally challenged or overwhelmed by transition events or nonevents? Which kinds of "stress" challenge you? Overwhelm you?
- Do you generally approach transitions as a fighting spirit, a stoic, a denier, a helpless person, or a believer in magic?
- Do you generally feel a sense of control or mastery as you face transitions? Do you usually balance mastery and pleasure?
- Do you usually face life as an optimist or pessimist?
- Do you know yourself?

Your *Supports*

No matter how strong our inner resources are, they are often not enough to guarantee that we can cope with a transition successfully. Most of us need the support of others to help us.

I understand this better now than I did when I was trying to be supportive to Steve, who had lost both his job and his wife in a short period of time. As I look back on what happened to him, I wonder how I could have been so matter-of-fact about his transitions. Of course, I was sympathetic and made the appropriate number of visits and phone calls. But I know now that I did not feel what must have been the depth of his loss. I did not realize that the loss of support and intimacy, coupled with his fear of diminishing options because of his sex and age, made him feel that he had lost everything that had given meaning to his life.

Another person who came to realize the importance of *Support* is Pat, whose transition began when her good friend had a stroke at the age of forty. Pat began to think, "If my friend is incapacitated, it could happen to me or my husband. If something happened to my husband, I am not prepared to support my family of six children." Around the same time, Pat's interest was piqued by a newspaper ad for a Women's External Degree program. Since the program required only occasional weekends on campus, she began to think that it might be possible for her to complete the degree she had begun years ago and to prepare herself to be self-supporting. Pat's husband, Bob, was very supportive when they talked about the idea of her returning to school. But when she did it, the reality that Pat was actually gone for three days at a time every six weeks irritated Bob, and he began to complain and even ridicule her. But Pat was so determined to complete the degree that she asked her mother to move in during the times she was away. Although Bob's support was eroding, the support of her mother and of the program made up for her husband's ambivalence.

Pat's case demonstrates that even when people are in fairly stable relationships, we cannot assume that those close to them will be totally supportive if they undergo a transition. In interviews about support we now ask, "In what ways is X supportive of you or your activities? In what ways, if any, does X subvert or sabotage your activities?" What we find is that support is often a double-edged sword. In many instances support is given in exchange for some measure of control. The unwritten statement is "I'll support you, but you need to behave as I think you should."

Some people give support but in a way that is not helpful. One woman wrote in a paper for one of my classes, "My boyfriend of five years told me he was one step away from being in love with another woman. This called into question all past assumptions I had about our relationship. I began to doubt myself." When we asked what helped her cope, she said, "Professional counseling." When asked if she had tried methods that were unhelpful, she replied, "Simply talking with friends. They could not understand—they were too biased. Their reactions ranged from pity for me to total anger. Although my friends meant well, they were ineffective." This is a case where friends did not give the kind of support that she felt she needed.

We can probably all agree that we all need support, but this is a very general concept. As a way to get a handle on it, I will describe what it is and where it comes from, and then show you how to visualize your own *Support* as you move through, tackle, face, or master your transitions.

Support—What It Is

We all have a visceral sense of what the word *support* means, of what we seek from friends, relatives, church, neighbors, co-workers, or even strangers. But understanding the functions of support—why it is important to us—is a bit more complicated.

Psychologist George Caplan defines support systems as ways that help individuals mobilize their resources to master change by sharing "tasks" and providing "extra supplies of money, materials, tools, skills," and by giving guidance about ways to improve coping.[8] Robert Kahn and Toni Antonucci have identified three key functions of support: affect, affirmation, and aid.[9] Let's look at what they mean:

- *Affect*—an expression that someone respects, likes, or loves you
- *Affirmation*—an expression that someone agrees that what you have done is appropriate or understandable
- *Assistance* or *aid*—an expression that someone will actually supply you with chicken soup, information, time, or whatever tangible help is necessary to get you over the crisis.

Where It Comes From

People receive affect, affirmation, and aid in many ways, from many sources. Sometimes they receive support from friends, but in other instances it comes from a professional. People can potentially get support from many sources: intimates, families, friends, strangers, and institutions. However, there are many times when these sources of support are not helpful. You, the person in transition, need to evaluate what kind of support you need—affect, affirmation, aid—and from what source you could receive it—friend, partner, stranger, or institution. Do you need support from one constant source, or would it help to have the comfort of a group of people who face similar problems? Today many people join self-help groups where they both give and receive support.

Intimates. We often extol the virtues of an intimate relationship, but sometimes the person with whom we are most intimate cannot be our best support. The men whose jobs were eliminated, for example, resisted going to their wives, mostly because they felt guilty about inflicting this transition on their families. In one extreme case, a man actually dressed and pretended to go to work. His wife didn't discover this until the unemployment checks began to arrive.

Despite these examples, most research confirms the importance of having an intimate—someone with whom to share honestly and openly your inner world. Intimates are extremely important during transitions. Intimate support comes in several packages: the intimacy you can achieve with friends who are often part of your adult life; the intimacy you can achieve with your spouse or partner; and the more permanent intimacy you get from parents, siblings, and children.

Family. Family can be a key source for giving and receiving affect, affirmation, assistance—and, at times, honest feedback. In most of our lives, the "forever" relationships are intergenerational, between grandparents, parents, and children. Without wanting to glorify these relationships (because they, like all others, are fraught with ambivalence and stress as well as support), we realize that they are central to our feelings of well-being. As we live longer, an increasing number of us continue to be part of four- or five-generation families. As sociologist Hagestad observes, "These family patterns, unprecedented in human history, have in a way taken our society by surprise. . . . Families today may have to sort out who gives help and support to whom when two generations face aging problems.[10] One woman was just about to retire when her mother became depressed and moved in with her. The daughter was not happy about the prospect of spending her retirement years with her mother since there had always been friction between them. But she says, although she might have been aggravated, she wasn't lonely. Most studies show that adult children stay in touch with their aging parents and that family members constitute the greatest sources of assistance to one another.

Friends. Support from friends, lovers, and partners also helps buffer stress, but the type of support they provide may differ from that provided by the family. As Lillian Rubin found in her study of friendships, "Friends help in the lifelong process of self-development, often becoming . . . people who join us in the journey toward maturity, who facilitate our separation from the family and encourage our developing individuality."

Thus, she points out, "one of the most valued gifts friends offer us [is]—a reflection of the self we most want to be. In the family it's different. There, it's our former selves that are entrenched in both the family's vision and our own." Rubin points to the changing functions and roles of friends and asserts that it is important to have a number of different types of intimates. She had found from countless interviews that "even when people are comfortably and happily married, the absence of friends exacts a heavy cost in loneliness and isolation."[11]

Strangers. When Rodney, a community organizer, found he had cancer, he fought it with all the energy he could muster. He went to the best doctors and even became part of a research experiment, but he went through physical and mental agony. His wife and adult children were totally supportive, and he also benefited from the support of a set of very close friends who had known the family since college days.

At the time of his diagnosis, Rodney was negotiating a major grant from a foundation. When the foundation learned that he had cancer, the negotiations fell apart. The feeling that he would now have to face a financial crisis on top of a life-threatening disease devastated Rodney. He explained the situation to his doctor, a relative stranger, who wrote a letter to the foundation explaining the circumstances of Rodney's disease and suggesting that the foundation would be discriminating if it did not provide the funds. As a result of the letter, the foundation's decision was reversed and Rodney received the grant. This case illustrates the necessity of having access to a variety of types of support—support from intimates, from friends, and from strangers.

A professional woman who lives in Washington, D.C., went to Denver to make a speech. When she arrived at the hotel where the meeting was scheduled, she learned that she was one month early. Unable to comprehend that she had done this, she was momentarily very upset. To compensate, she decided to treat herself to a lovely lunch at one of the best restaurants in town. The maître d' was friendly, and the woman found herself telling him about her terrible error. He laughed and told her about a mistake he had made. This interchange with a stranger was enormously helpful, and by the time lunch was over, she had regained her humor and perspective.

Institutions and organizations. One woman describes how she coped with widowhood: "Not only was the transition off-time, but it was unanticipated and outside my control, so there was a high degree of stress. This was balanced by an environment of tremendous social support from family, friends, and my department at work. I could not have survived without the constant telephone calls, concern, and continuous offers of help. I was surprised at my initiative in creating a support group of single women to share common concerns."[12]

Many people do not have the energy to create a new, ad hoc, special support group. Fortunately, many existing organizations are already available to support us in times of change. There are many single-purpose organizations such as Alcoholics Anonymous (AA), where alcoholics offer advice and strength to others. The idea behind AA has been expanded to other special-purpose organizations, such as Gamblers Anonymous, Overeaters Anonymous, and, I am sure, many more such groups.

Other single-purpose groups have sprung up. These include Parents Without Partners, caretakers of those with Alzheimer's disease, and parents of disabled children, including those with learning disabilities, mental illness, and physical illness.

More general are institutions such as Family Services, Red Cross, Travelers Aid, and the various social welfare and counseling arms of religious, ethnic, and national groups.

Then, of course, there are a host of organizations created to deal with the special problems of women, Hispanics, blacks, immigrants, the foreign born, gays, and other segments of the population that have not been getting their share of support from this society.

In addition, there are organizations such as unions and professional business and trade groups. And last, but certainly not least, are the churches that offer formal services in addition to the tremendous resource of the "people power" of fellow congregants, who can and do become helpers at least and friends at best.

Whether you are facing a troubling situation or initiating a desired change, the support from institutions can be invaluable.

Different Supports *for Men and Women.* The support networks and intimate relationships available to us depend on many factors—where we live, our age, our economic status, our own personality. But some research suggests that sex is a particularly important determinant of the composition of one's network of *Supports.* This stems from the changing sex ratio over the course of life. Men and women live in somewhat different worlds. Although more boys are born than girls, by the time people are in their mid-thirties, there are more women than men. This imbalance has resulted in remarriage becoming a disproportionately male experience after age forty. By the time people are in their eighties, there are more than twice as many women as men. Thus the majority of older women are widowed and have a social life with other women, while most older men are married and have a social life with couples.

The types of *Supports* we need and can offer may change depending on our age and circumstances. The demographics of age and sex may impinge on our ability to get the type of *Supports* we need at the time we need them. Hagestad's interviews with grandparents, middle-aged men, and women and their adult children suggest that men's ups and downs are tied more often to the world of work and politics, while women's are related more to events in the family. Further, she found that when men get together, they talk about work, education, money, and social issues, while women focus more on interpersonal relations and family.[13]

Support for the Supporter. Often we forget that a person who is giving support to a friend or family member in need may also require some support to help shoulder the additional burden. We can see this in the case of Sarah, who confided to her brother Mark that she was having her second abortion and swore him to secrecy. Mark became Sarah's rock through the trauma, although it was extremely difficult for him since his political and philosophical views about the morality of abortion were in flux at the time of Sarah's confidence. Because Mark loved Sarah, he stuck by her and didn't tell her about his own changing views. In addition, he couldn't confide in any of his friends about the stress of being Sarah's supporter because this was Sarah's secret. Mark was helping Sarah to cope, but he needed support so that he could continue being the supporter.

Another example is Adele, a woman whose best friend's baby died. Adele's role was coordinating the funeral and friends' visits. She reported that she had no time to mourn the loss herself and felt very stressed by her coordinating role. She, too, felt a need for tender loving care.

To summarize: We all need support and can get it from many types of people—friends, family, colleagues, neighbors, parents, and children.

But because life is by definition a series of transitions for all of us, the specific individuals with whom we have supportive relationships change as life unfolds, and the options for relationships also change. We also require different *types* of support at different times.

A Way to Visualize the Range of Your Supports

Kahn and Antonucci have developed a way for you to identify your potential *Supports* by drawing a series of concentric circles

Figure 4–1. Your "Convoy of Social Support"

Convoy membership: tied directly to role relationship, and most vulnerable to role changes (like a co-worker with whom you are not very close)

Convoy membership: some-what role related and likely to change over time

Convoy membership: stable over time and no longer role dependent

Close family (You) Close friends

Partner

Family, relatives

Neighbors

Co-workers

Supervisors

Professionals (doctors, lawyers, dentists)

Friends (work, neighborhood)

Distant family

Source: Based on work from "Convoys over the Life Course: Attachment, Roles, and Social Support," by R.L. Kahn and T.C. Antonucci, in *Life-Span Development and Behavior,* edited by P.B. Baltes and O.C. Brim, Jr. (New York: Academic Press, 1980), p. 273. Reprinted by permission.

with you at the center (see figure 4–1). The circle closest to you contains your closest, most intimate friends and family, who are presumably part of your life forever. The next circle is for family, friends, and neighbors who are important in your life but not in the intimate way the first group is. The circle farthest away from you represents more institutional supports. Kahn and Antonucci call these circles an individual's "convoy of social support," which he or she carries through life.[14]

Actually mapping out your *Supports* in concentric circles in this method enables you to see how much a transition interrupts or increases your support system. For example, geographical moves can interrupt relationships between husbands and wives. Spouses who do not want to move but who agree to do so for the sake of the family may harbor deep resentment and anger. Thus, a wife who follows her husband may have had him in the center of her life before the move, but she may shift him to one of the more distant circles after it. In a contrasting case, a new college administrator reports that his wife is delighted with their move back to Washington, D.C., because she lived there before and has a large support network in the city. If we were to compare her concentric circles before and after the move, her husband's place would be the same—in the closest circle.

Other examples can be readily found by looking at what happens to people's support systems before and after retirement. If a newly retired couple moves away from many *Supports* to a place with none, the transition may be very difficult. If, however, retirement liberates one of the spouses to move back to an area where there are intimate relatives and friends, then it might be a much easier transition. This system of concentric circles shows that the most important aspect of a transition may not be the change itself but what it does to the individual's "convoy."

In summary: To take stock of your *Supports* you can ask yourself,

- Am I getting what I need for this transition in terms of affect? Affirmation? Aid?
- Do I have a range of types of support—spouse or partner, other close family or friends, co-workers/colleagues/neighbors, organizations, strangers, and institutions?
- Has my support system or "convoy of social support" been interrupted by this transition?
- Do I feel my support system for this transition is a low or a high resource?

Putting It Together: The Case of David

An analysis of the experience of David, a top administrator in the
state highway patrol, illustrates the importance of TAKING
STOCK of the three factors we have been discussing in this part
of the book: your *Situation,* your inner resources or *Self,* and your
Supports.

After twenty-seven years in the state highway patrol, David
decided to return to school to earn a degree that would enable him
to become a teacher when he retired. Full of enthusiasm, he
enrolled in a state university. To all appearances David was a
responsible, dedicated professional who had identified teaching as
a means of making the transition to a second career in his retirement years. Yet two years and a lot of hard work later, he dropped
out of school without finishing the requirements for the degree. "I
feel disappointment, some resentment, and at times anger," he
said after the experience. "I usually achieve what I start out to
achieve."

What went wrong? David thought he had accumulated enough
credits to graduate by taking courses at the university and by
enrolling in a program designed to evaluate prior experience and,
if appropriate, award credit. The process of applying for such
credit is complicated and requires the learner to develop a detailed
portfolio of each experience. David applied for his B.A. degree,
only to discover that although he had enough credits, many were
from community college courses, and he did not have enough
from the university. When he realized that he still needed sixty
more credits that had to be taken on the campus, David became
infuriated and dropped out of school.

In order to understand what happened, let's TAKE STOCK of
David's *Situation, Self,* and *Supports.* In the next chapter we can
TAKE STOCK of his *Strategies.*

TAKING STOCK of David's Situation

There were many pluses in David's *Situation.* The transition was
one he had elected, and he was beginning to see himself as someone who could make his career dreams come true. On the negative

side were his changed routines requiring that he drive ninety miles each way twice a week. He had to think through his plans for each week and find time to study as well as to work and be with his family. David felt that his family was getting the short end of the stick. But overall he was pleased about the transition to learner and evaluated it very positively.

TAKING STOCK of David's Self

David describes himself as a "hard worker," a "go-getter." He classifies himself as a "fighting spirit," and an "optimist," but he adds, "If things don't go the way I think they should, I can fly off the handle. Maybe I am a little short on patience." So David may be his own best and worst resource. He fights for what he wants and believes in, but he may give up if the odds seem unfavorable.

TAKING STOCK of David's Supports

David assesses his family support as "terrific." His wife took on additional family responsibilities so that he could give his all to getting his degree. He also feels positively about his co-workers' support. Some teased him about going to school, but mostly they thought it was great. He was getting a good supply of affect, affirmation, and aid.

David's downfall was his perceived lack of institutional support. He claims he never received information about the credit limitations from outside institutions. The dean claims that David was informed but was so eager that he didn't pay attention to advice to slow down. Whatever the facts, there was clearly a breakdown in communication—a breakdown that prompted David to leave.

In sum, David's *Situation, Self,* and *Supports* all had positive and negative aspects.

By TAKING STOCK of the *Situation, Self,* and *Supports* of David and others described in these two chapters, we have illustrated two crucial insights into the transition process:

- That both *Self* and *Supports* generally offer both positives and negatives in terms of our preparation for and ability to deal with a transition
- That as much or more than the transition itself, what determines our success is *how we evaluate* the transition and our resources for coping with it.

* * * * *

Your *Self* Review

- Are you generally challenged rather than over-   Yes   No
whelmed by transitions?
- Do you generally feel a sense of control or   Yes   No
mastery as you face transitions?
- Do you usually face life as an optimist rather   Yes   No
than as a pessimist?
- Do you define yourself as resilient in the face   Yes   No
of change?
- Taking all of the above into account, do you rate
your *Self* as:

A high resource	Yes	No
A low resource	Yes	No
A mixed bag	Yes	No
Okay	Yes	No

* * * * *

Your *Support* Review

- Are you getting what you need for this tran-   Yes   No
sition in terms of:

Affect?	Yes	No
Affirmation?	Yes	No
Aid?	Yes	No

- Do you have a range of types of support—   Yes   No
  spouse or partner, other close family or friends,
  co-workers/colleagues/neighbors, organizations,
  strangers?
- Have you checked the institutions that are avail-   Yes   No
  able to you?
- Has your "convoy of social support"—from   Yes   No
  intimate to institution—been interrupted by this
  transition?
- Do you regard your *Support* for this transi-   Yes   No
  tion as:
  - A high resource   Yes   No
  - A low resource   Yes   No
  - A mixed bag   Yes   No
  - Okay   Yes   No

5

TAKING STOCK of your
Strategies

I T'S easy to identify things that upset you; what's hard is decid-
ing what to do about your feelings and the situations that give
rise to them. Confronting very challenging transitions often makes
people feel helpless and therefore hopeless. They may feel that
they have little control over their *Situation* and that their options
are few. But in fact there are almost always more *Strategies* than
people realize. Sociologist Leonard Pearlin tells us that there is no
single, magic-bullet coping strategy. The effective coper is someone who can use many *Strategies* flexibly, depending on the *Situation.* You already have a repertoire of coping *Strategies* that have
helped you in the past. But when the going gets tough, you may
well need to expand them further.

To help you TAKE STOCK of your coping repertoire, I will
present an array of coping *Strategies* in this chapter. I have drawn
them from the work of experts like Pearlin and colleagues who
study coping and from the wisdom and experience of friends, students, and people I have interviewed and counseled.

On the basis of interviews with 2,300 people between eighteen
and sixty-five living in the Chicago area, Pearlin and Schooler
identified the major coping strategies people used as they faced
life's strains and joys.[1] They distinguished three types of coping
strategies: those that *change the situation,* those that *change its
meaning,* and those that *help you relax.* Based on the work of

Richard Lazarus, I added a fourth; knowing when to *do nothing* or *take deliberate inaction.*[2]

Having a variety of coping strategies in mind can help you expand and diversify; it both helps you identify those you already use and suggests new ones to try.

One of my graduate students, Geraldine, describes how having a wide repertoire of coping strategies has helped her succeed despite her learning disability. She relates this story:

> My parents love to tell stories about the "cute" way I used to confuse words. For example, I would say "bowel" for "elbow." However, I view learning disabilities a little differently.
>
> School was a place where I was often reprimanded for getting directions confused and not listening the first time. I failed home economics because the only test of the semester involved labeling all thirty or so parts of the sewing machine. French was a farce: I could comprehend it when I read it, but the teacher would laugh hysterically when I spoke sentences in French. Geometry would have been fine if I could have used a mirror. Although I have learned to compensate in many ways, I still become frustrated when I have to reread paragraphs because of reversals and transpositions.
>
> As I studied the coping skills described by Pearlin and Schooler, I realized how many I used in my own life. It is probably because I use so many strategies that I am now a graduate student. Here are some of the major strategies I used:
>
> - *Negotiation:* I learned by the time I was in high school to identify a supportive teacher and have her (usually a woman) negotiate on my behalf. For example, one teacher negotiated with the history teacher and I was allowed to tape my history class.
> - *Optimistic Action:* I became a reading specialist so I could first help myself and now can help many others by serving as an advocate for learning-disabled children.
> - *Advice-seeking:* I really drained many professionals as I sought expert advice; their assistance was extremely helpful.
> - *Positive Comparisons:* When I received my Graduate Record Examination scores I was devastated by the mundane results. I

was overwhelmed by a feeling of stupidity. Then I thought about some of the bizarre things that have happened and I said to myself: "Damn, but look how far you have come!"

- *Selective Ignoring:* I often say, "Who cares if you don't know east from west, read slowly, and write backwards, as long as you are motivated and productive."
- *Emotional Release:* I play lots of racquet ball, often screaming to let off steam.
- *Other Strategies:* I am well-organized, am part of an extremely strong and caring support group, and I'm proficient at networking to find individuals who can assist me.

I agree with Geraldine; she is a master of diverse coping strategies, and that mastery has paid off handsomely in helping her achieve despite her disability. You can expand your own repertoire by using some of the strategies described here. But first you need to TAKE STOCK of your own *Strategies* so that you can see your usual approach to coping.

Strategies to Change or Modify the Transition

All of us confront situations that we want to change. You probably have some typical ways of trying to alter things. Maybe it's through negotiating or taking direct action. But there are other strategies, too, including seeking advice, asserting yourself, brainstorming to develop an alternative plan, or even taking legal action when needed. Have you used all of these?

Negotiating

You can sometimes turn a no-win situation into a winning one by negotiating: by sitting down, talking things through, seeing the other person's assumptions and point of view, and trying to meet everyone's needs. We are always negotiating, but some people are better at it than others, and some people learn how to improve their negotiating skills through training. People can learn and apply such skills in many areas, including labor-management relations, supervisor-supervisee relations, couple relationships, and parent-child relationships.

Gerard I. Nierenberg, president of the Negotiation Institute, puts the definition and potential of negotiation well. He writes:

> Nothing could be simpler in definition or broader in scope than negotiation. Every desire that demands satisfaction—and every need to be met—is at least potentially an occasion for people to initiate the negotiating process. Whenever people exchange ideas with the intention of changing relationships, whenever they confer for agreement, they are negotiating.[3]

Stephanie's story illustrates the importance of negotiating in changing a situation. She writes:

> My transitions relate to my eye problems. I had severe and pervasive eye hemorrhages. My already poor vision was almost lost entirely for two months. I was helped to cope by several things. First, when I realized that I was becoming legally blind, I went to a career counselor. As a result of that, I began taking courses so I could shift to a type of work that made fewer demands on my eyesight.
>
> Second, when this latest incident occurred, I called my boss and began negotiating a way to change my work assignment. I explained my needs and recognized his. To meet his needs, I tried to figure out the parts of the job I could do without top vision.

Taking Optimistic Action

There are times when people are in a situation they define as negative, but instead of wallowing in it, they take some action to solve the problem and try to find a solution. They stick at it, never giving in to those tempting feelings of helplessness. That's optimistic action.

Some families with chronically ill children use this strategy frequently. They constantly seek out new information on the illness and try to keep their home situation and their child's life as normal as possible. Taking action keeps the family mobilized.

Seeking Advice

Many people feel that they must shoulder a difficult situation themselves; it's somehow dishonorable to lean on others. But in fact, seeking advice is a very useful coping strategy. Sometimes, just talking with someone close can help you think through your situation; at other times, expert advice may be needed.

One example of advice seeking as a coping strategy comes from Renee. A factory worker, she received a note from her husband one day saying that he had packed up and left. She couldn't believe that she had been abandoned; she had little money and three children to support, and she felt she was in an unbearable situation.

She says she felt utterly empty, "as if someone had taken my insides and torn them out of me." As she sat in front of me with tears in her eyes, recalling that moment, I asked, "How did you survive?" "My situation was unbelievable," she answered. "It was out of my control, stressful, horrible. But I had two things going for me. First, I had the support of three kids who comforted me at the beginning and pushed me to take a secretarial course so I could get a better job. Second, I became good at finding resources, like the lawyer who helped me for no money. My ability to seek advice helped me find the counselor who told me to join a support group and to keep a diary of everything that was said. Knowing how to seek advice and uncover resources is critical for coping with a situation that needs changing."

Asserting Yourself

Exercising your right to stand up for yourself and say no without feeling guilty is essential for mental health and coping. The skill of asserting yourself effectively can help you through daily hassles as well as major transitions. For example, Joan, a shy young woman, felt "put upon" because Amy, her roommate, expected Joan to type her papers. Grateful for Amy's friendship and afraid of losing it, Joan did the typing but with great resentment.

After a course on assertiveness training at a local recreation center, Joan learned how to empathize with Amy: "I understand your need to have papers typed." But she also learned how to say no: "However, typing your papers makes me feel resentful, something I don't think is good for our relationship. Why don't you hire a typist?"

This strategy is so much better than screaming, "You always impose on me and I'm sick of it!" Learning to say no without feeling guilty can add an important skill to your coping repertoire.

Brainstorming a New Plan

When faced with a challenging situation, many people feel trapped and stymied because they lack new ways of problem solving. Sometimes it helps to brainstorm, alone or with someone else. You simply let your ideas flow, generating all the suggestions or solutions you can think of, without censoring them or judging whether they make sense or could really work. After you note as many suggestions as you can generate, then you sit down and think carefully through the pros and cons of each one. The important thing is to turn off your critical judgment at first, so your ideas can develop.

I was very surprised a few years ago when James, a casual friend of my husband's, invited us to brunch. I was even more surprised when the purpose became clear. James and his wife, Debbie, had invited only the two of us. It was the first time I had ever met them. Before we ate, they toured us through their very attractive apartment, decorated with great taste and flair. Then, at the elegant brunch table, James announced that he had been very depressed about his dead-end job; in fact, he felt on the verge of suicide.

We both listened sympathetically as he and his wife described their desperation, the continual appointments with new psychiatrists, the medications that never seemed to help. Finally, they explained, they had decided to invite people over to explore new directions he might take in his career.

We suggested a number of options, including volunteer work. Every one met with "That's a good idea, but it's not practical" or "That really doesn't interest me." We were stymied; they had asked for our help and our empathic listening, yet they had not really wanted either.

Finally I commented on how frustrating our inability to help must feel to them. Then I pointed out how creative they had been in decorating their bedroom. The bed, for example, had been placed in the center of the room, not against the wall. They agreed that it was an offbeat arrangement and said that they had tried many others before hitting on this.

Something clicked in my head. I suggested that since they had solved a decorating problem by being willing to explore many options, the same approach might work in thinking about James's career. Somehow this hit home. They acknowledged their resistance, and we began to brainstorm together in earnest, developing a long list of career options for James to consider—some wild and improbable, some very conventional. I don't know if James used any of the specific suggestions the four of us came up with that day. But I recently learned that he is in a completely new line of work and loves it.

I am not saying that there are always unlimited opportunities to be or do anything you choose. Remember when women couldn't be astronauts; when blacks couldn't be college presidents, except at black institutions; when homosexuals couldn't hold high government positions; and when people over sixty-five couldn't hold jobs in most organizations? Although at times certain options really are closed, there are usually many ways to manage and create opportunities if we just let ourselves imagine them. Brian's story puts it all in perspective.

In one disastrous moment, a car accident transformed Brian, an athletic young man, into a paraplegic. At first he wanted to give up and die. "What's the use of living?" he asked himself. Then he became angry, first at himself for falling asleep at the wheel, then at "God" for letting this happen to him. Eventually, he began to fight to stay alive and to find meaning in his life. But it didn't happen overnight.

It took a year of hard work before Brian was able to leave the hospital and move home. It took another year to become accustomed to a whole new routine—doing hours of physical exercise each day, learning how to manipulate a wheelchair and how to drive a car. During that year he broke up with his lover and moved out on his own.

In addition to concentrating on managing his body and his day-to-day living, Brian needed to figure out what to do with his life. He had been a carpenter working for a building contractor; clearly he could no longer do that. What other options did he have? At first he felt he had none—that his life was over. Gradually, he began to think he could be a productive person. He realized that he could live his life as a loser and a victim or he could, as he wrote his mother, "face my future with hope, courage, and curiosity." He chose the latter, reframing his situation and looking at it with curiosity. What changes could he initiate that would make his life meaningful?

The answer came on a ten-hour plane trip to the National Conference for the Disabled, when Brian discovered that planes have no space for wheelchairs to fit into toilets. As a result, he had a very humiliating experience on that flight. But that experience convinced him that architects and designers are needed who understand the problems of the disabled, and he decided then to become an architect, interior designer, or draftsman so he could help others like himself.

Brian had survived a horrible accident; he had broken up a long-standing relationship; and he developed a plan for a new, useful career. Although his body is not whole, he is a whole person. He created, uncovered, and discovered sides to himself that he never knew he had and options that he had never imagined. This is not meant to romanticize tragedy but merely to point out the endlessly possible ways to live a life.

Strategies to Change the Meaning of the Transition

There are times when you simply can't change a situation: you didn't receive tenure, your plant closed, your best friend moved away, you have suffered a debilitating accident. But there are several ways you can alter the meaning of a situation. Let's look at some of them.

Applying Knowledge of the Transition Process

One of the basic tenets of this book is that transitions alter your life and require a period of adjustment—often several years. Remember my story about my family's move into a condominium? My husband and I sold the family home and moved into a condo before our son had really left home and before we had originally expected to do it.

Some of the difficulty arose because the timing was bad for our son. But even with better planning and timing, the move would have been disruptive because the beginning of any transition is quite stressful. We needed to understand that our reactions were quite normal, that we *all* feel at sea anytime our routines and assumptions are changed.

In chapter 2, I also told the story of Lisa, who moved to take a great new job and join her lover. A year after the move she was depressed and still couldn't get her feelings together, despite all the pluses. Lisa's case raises a critical point. When a major disruption occurs, the transition process requires a great deal of adaptation, even when the benefits far outweigh the deficits. In other words, even though the move was positive, Lisa had still changed her daily and monthly routines, her worker role, and some of her assumptions about herself. Transitions are usually much easier for people who have ample coping resources than they are for people with very limited resources. But people in both situations can be helped by knowing about the transition process. Of course, the process and its pain are still there, but understanding can cut down on some of the upset.

I am reminded of Lynn Caine, author of the book *Widow*.[4] She wrote that she wished someone had told her that there would be an end to the agony of bereavement. She said it wouldn't have eased the pain or the mourning over her husband's death, but it would have been comforting to know that someday she would move past the despair she felt. Suddenly widowed, she had abruptly moved to an area where she knew no one (and where driving was a necessity, but she had no license). In other words, knowledge of the transition process can ease one's pain and provide a time perspective.

Rehearsing the Transition

Psychologist Bernice Neugarten describes the importance of rehearsing for transitions—trying to visualize exactly how you would behave if an expected transition occurred. She has discovered that in later life men often rehearse for retirement and women for widowhood.

Rehearsing includes thinking about, even discussing, one's projected transition. For example, where will you live when you retire? What will you wear when you get up in the morning? How will you structure your day? Such rehearsals help people cope with the events when they really happen. It is harder to deal with transitions when they are ''off-time''—for example, when retirement comes early because of an unexpected plant closing, or when a young spouse is accidentally killed—partly because people don't rehearse for such situations.[5]

My family had decided in a very short time to sell the big house and move. This gave us no time to rehearse. But an increasing number of people who retire to the Sun Belt rehearse the move by living in their new locale for a winter before relocating there permanently.

Developing Rituals

Transitions are sometimes easier to accept when they are accompanied by rituals. Weddings, christenings, and farewell parties are all rituals that ease our transitions. But many important transitions do not have established rituals, and people may have to create their own. The importance of rituals can be seen in the story of Janet, who at age eighteen announced to her parents that instead of staying at home and attending the local junior college, she had decided to go to work and move into her own apartment.

Her shocked parents felt rejected. They had given her a good home. Why was she leaving it? And how would they cope with this unexpected transition? There was no accepted ritual to help them deal with having an eighteen-year-old move out of the house.

Coincidentally, Janet's parents heard the late anthropologist

Barbara Myerhoff discuss the importance of ritual in helping people deal with "marginal periods"—when they are shifting from one phase of life to another. She described the many significant events and nonevents that we fail to ritualize. She even used the case of eighteen-year-olds moving out.

Janet's parents took Myerhoff's presentation seriously and decided to ritualize Janet's departure by giving a celebration dinner and inviting their closest family friends. They chose gifts and wrote poems to commemorate her past and celebrate her future. They even promised to pay for phone installation, which would connect Janet to her past—but they expected her to pay the monthly phone charges. This helped them all handle the transition.

How does one develop rituals for what many people consider to be nonevents? For example, rituals abound for marriage, but there are very few rituals for those who choose not to marry. In the November 1984 *Ms.* magazine, a fascinating article appeared, entitled "Rites of Independence: New Ceremonies for New People."[6] It reproduced an announcement that a woman sent to friends to celebrate her singlehood:

> *Alice and Carl Hesse*
> *are pleased to announce their daughter*
> *Susan A. Hesse*
> *is settling into*
> *Joyous Old Maidhood*
> *after which she shall cease*
> *looking for Mr. Right*
> *and begin giving*
> *scintillating dinner parties and soirées.*
>
> *To help celebrate this wonderful occasion*
> *gift place-settings*
> *are available at*
> *Macy's Department Store. . . .*

Myerhoff created and used films to teach people how to come up with rituals that "punctuate and clarify" critical times in their lives. The divorce ritual in one film, *Rites of Renewal,* does just that.[7] The minister calls together the divorcing couple and has them repeat an oath of caring but unconnecting. He then asks them to pledge their care, concern, and love for their child even though their love for each other has vanished. He finally includes the couple's parents and friends in the ceremony. Many who watch this film cry during this sequence, probably because we have all been intimately connected with such wrenching splits. Coming up with rituals for your own events or nonevents may be both a creative challenge and comfort.

Making Positive Comparisons *("Count Your Blessings")*

Leonard Pearlin notes that people tend to judge the severity of their situations by comparing them with the situations of people close to them. I keep remembering Blanche, a woman in a nursing home who had Lou Gehrig's disease (an illness that eventually obliterates all muscle function). She could barely talk or swallow, and she had lost all movement of her arms and legs. But one day she said to me, "Bad as this is, at least I don't have to be tube fed."

One psychologist at the University of California at Los Angeles studied how women react to their breast cancer. She found that most of the women "chose to compare themselves to other patients who were . . . more seriously ill. When patients did not know an actual person who was worse off, they invented an imaginary one. For example, patients who had one lump removed pitied women who had undergone full mastectomies. . . . Even women who were very seriously ill found relief in the knowledge that they were not dying or were not in pain." The point "is that they make the right comparison."[8]

Rearranging Priorities

One way to cope with a difficult transition is to define the aspect of your life in which you are stressed as less important to you than other aspects of your life. A person frustrated in a job area may decide that love, family, and community service are what really matter and that work is just a way to earn a living. If the stress is in the family area, then work may become a top priority.

Some of the men my colleagues and I interviewed whose jobs had been eliminated were devastated because their work was critical to their sense of selfhood. They were unable to devalue the job and play up some other aspects of their lives. But one of the men, a grass cutter, said that his job was not that important to him. In fact, he said, if he didn't work, his wife would go back to being a cook and he would care for the children—an activity he always enjoyed.

Redefining priorities often happens spontaneously as a way of coping. It's harder to do it deliberately, but it can be done if you step back mentally from the stressful situation and try to see which other areas of your life also matter a lot to you. One way to size up their importance is to ask yourself how you'd feel if they, too, were severely disrupted.

Relabeling: The Process of Redefining the Transition

According to psychologist Richard Lazarus, people spontaneously size up and label their current situation as irrelevant, positive, or stressful. They also assess their ability and resources to cope with the situation. But these definitions can be changed. Relabeling occurs when you redefine either the situation or your ability to cope with it.

Earlier I described the celebration ritual for Janet, the young woman who moved into her own apartment—a transition her parents had initially viewed as very stressful. After listening to an anthropologist's speech, Janet's parents relabeled the transition as positive; instead of regarding Janet's departure as a rejection, they started to see it as part of growing up.

Selective Ignoring

Some people use "selective ignoring" to help them cope. When faced with a troublesome situation, they may play down the bad parts and play up the good.

Many partnerships flounder because one partner notices every bad habit of the other. After two divorces, one man reported that counseling had helped him realize that he had focused on all the negative habits of his former wives. He began to see that focusing on the positives and not looking for perfection makes for a much better relationship. This strategy, however, like several others cited above, is easier said than done. It can, however, be learned and added to your repertoire—as the story of Beth, the single mother of two teenagers, illustrates.

Beth knows she is a "direct-action" person. If something goes wrong, she negotiates and asserts herself. If she needs help, she'll call everyone she knows to find the appropriate resource. Her coping style has helped her through many difficult times, but it has sometimes been a hindrance to her in managing her teenagers.

When Sherry, her sixteen-year-old daughter, started driving, Beth was always on her case. If Sherry came home one minute late, Beth would be at the door, almost pouncing on her. This inevitably provoked a fight and failed to encourage Sherry to be more prompt. Then Beth learned about "selective ignoring" in a course, and she decided to try it out with Sherry.

Clearly, Beth cannot and should not ignore a lateness of two hours. But ten minutes is another story. By deliberately not "noticing" everything, Beth is giving a message of confidence to Sherry. But more important, she has added another *strategy* to her coping repertoire.

Beth reports that all was going well until Rick, her fourteen-year-old son, perceived that his mother was being more lenient with Sherry. Then Rick started nagging Beth, accusing her of being too easy on her daughter. Beth concludes her story with a laugh, saying, "You never can win!"

Denial

We have grown up thinking that good mental health and facing reality go hand in hand. Lately, though, a surge of research has been pointing out that some types of denial—not facing the facts or minimizing them—can be beneficial.

Psychiatrist George Vaillant distinguishes between *immature* and *mature* denial. In immature denial, for instance people redefine external reality in a false way by saying, when someone needs an operation, that surgery has no risks. In mature denial, people make a "conscious or semi-conscious decision to postpone paying attention" to a problem or reality. They are "postponing but not avoiding forever" dealing head-on with the problem.[9]

For some people, going into surgery armed with all the facts can be destructive and can lead to unnecessary anxiety. They might be more comfortable finding out what they need to know about the surgeon's competence but not every detail—every risk and consequence—before the operation. By minimizing or even suppressing their own awareness of the operation's potential pain and complications, they are better able to cope. Later, when they are in a better position to handle the information, they will find out about the results of the surgery.

Humor

When my colleagues and I interviewed people about how they cope, most of them did not spontaneously mention using humor as a strategy. But when we specifically asked about their use of humor, many could remember a time when it had worked. I asked members of a church group, "Have you ever used humor as a way to cope?" One person said, "Always! It helps to be able to see the silly, negative, stupid things I have done to contribute to a bad situation. Or to verbalize extremes. These extremes often lurk in your mind as fears, and turning them into humor depowers them."

Is having a sense of humor a strategy that can be taught, or is it a trait people either have or don't have? Carol Wade, also a psychologist, suggests a number of strategies that can be used to "improve your laugh life." This summary of some of her suggestions might be helpful as you try to increase your coping repertoire:

- Think of potentially stressful situations and prepare humorous responses.
- Search for the humor in a situation—even if it's a tragic one. For example, one woman, a computer programmer whose mother died and whose son and best friend were both diagnosed as having fatal diseases, called another friend one day and said with a laugh, "This is Jane, your representative of a multiproblem family." Laughing at smaller problems can help, too. A man who was just returning from a trip with gifts for his family lost his luggage. He quipped, "At least I don't have to unpack. Look at all the time I'm saving."
- Think of situations, books, and movies that make you laugh out loud.
- Look at the humor in what you are doing—try to laugh at yourself.

In trying to hone your sense of humor, it may be well to review what Wade claims are the three major purposes of humor:

- It helps you interpret a situation and distance yourself from it.
- It can help you get a sense of control over a situation.
- It acts as a way to let off steam and treat embarrassing or dangerous emotions in a funny, less emotionally charged way.[10]

Having Faith

Many of us find it important to reflect about ourselves, our world, and our place in it. We meditate, pray, read, and visit churches, temples, mosques—even psychics. Several recent articles have reported on stockbrokers, government officials, and others who visit psychics for a reading on a regular basis. One woman writes, "I think for many people God and their faith is an important part of their lives and can influence how they behave and perceive things. My perspective of life doesn't end at death but goes on forever."

On a recent cross-country plane trip I was sitting beside a very attractive, well-groomed woman who was reading her Bible. Toward the last hour of the flight we began to talk, and she told me her story. Her husband is in the navy; she has moved at least fifteen times since they married. I asked how she felt about moving, and she said she loves it. "It's really a challenge—it keeps me stretched," she said.

"How do you deal with all the changes?" I asked. She told me that until about six years ago she had lived her married life always trying to please everyone. If her husband yelled at her—and he often did—she wouldn't yell back. Even in the grocery line, she would try to please the cashier. She felt very bad that she was so insecure.

Then she had become involved with a fundamentalist church and had had an experience that changed her life: "a conversation with Jesus." She began to worry less about her own insecurity and began to approach people differently. Christ told her that her marriage was stagnant and that much of the problem was her own inability to be herself and be direct. She participated more in church and began to speak up more at home.

Finally she told her husband that while she did not expect him to change, she did expect him to accept her change. Since he did not seem able to do that, she decided to leave him. He was so astounded by this that he, too, joined the church, and their marriage was renewed. He no longer loses his temper, she said; he is now a better administrator in the navy and a much better husband and father. She feels that she can handle anything now because of her relationship with God and Jesus Christ. That feeling gave her the strength to make a radical change in her view of herself and in her subsequent behavior.

Another woman whose faith helped her cope explained her situation this way: "I was dealing with parents, in-laws, two adult children, a demanding husband, and my own desire to work. The pressures became great when my mother became critically ill and I had to travel frequently across the country, sometimes staying with her for weeks at a time. I managed by remembering how I had coped when my father-in-law was ill. I remembered that the way I did it was to take each day at a time, relying on faith.

''My religious beliefs are strong and very important to me. I realized that the life course is one in which there is an expectation of death, that I, too, will die. I just kept thinking how fulfilled my mother's life had been, how happy I was that I was well and could help her.''

Taking Stress in Your Stride: Managing Reactions to Stress

We have looked at strategies that help you change your situation or its meaning. But how do you deal with stress when it seems impossible to change or redefine the situation that is the source of the stress immediately? As you become more conscious of the effects of stress, you will learn to use strategies that help you relax so you can take the stress in stride. I will describe a number of strategies that people use, but you may have to experiment to find the ones that work best for you. Reading, for example, can be relaxing to one person but agitating to another. And to further complicate things, what can relax you at one time in your life or during one transition can stress you at another time.

In response to a questionnaire asking people how they cope with stressful situtions, one respondent almost covered the waterfront. She said she ''went into therapy, made new friends, attended a health spa for aerobics and massages, took a program in progressive relaxation and self-hypnosis, joined a singles group for support, and started doing 'fun' things like dancing.'' The list of possible strategies is much longer even than this and is extremely varied; playing, reading, using relaxation skills, meditating, imaging, using biofeedback, expressing emotions (through praying, crying, laughing, singing, chanting), relaxing through massage and spas, and doing physical exercise such as jogging, swimming, aerobics, and dancing are only a few common examples.

Playing

We normally think of playing as the province of children and gods and forget how crucial it is for adults. Dan Levitan, a physical education professor at the University of Maryland and director of an activity program for older adults, reports that fun and play are among the best buffers to stress. He had designed a simple but effective program for older people to help them play.

Each older person in the program is teamed with an undergraduate. Together they participate in enjoyable activities such as singing, dancing, and listening to lectures. My colleagues and I interviewed some of the older adults in his program. One man reported that he had been at the end of his rope. First his wife had died, then his only son. Somehow he had heard of the program, dragged himself over to the university, and to his amazement had started having fun and feeling again that he could find enjoyment and pleasure in his life. As he said, "The program literally saved my life."

People sometimes get so caught up in the strain of a transition that they forget to build fun and pleasure into their lives, or they feel they don't have time for fun. It may be impossible to go on your dream vacation, but there are many simpler, more accessible pleasures that are fun and that can help you to relax. One woman I know goes hat shopping when she needs a fun break. Another takes luxurious bubble baths. A neighbor gets some friends together for a round of poker. A cousin hits the road to explore the local antique shops. If you think about it a bit, you can come up with your own roster of small pleasures that are fun to do and that can fit into your most stressful period.

Emotional Release

Transitions often generate powerful emotional reactions: anxiety, anger, frustration, sadness, and more. Yet there's a strong streak of "stiff-upper-lip" philosophy in our culture that makes it hard for some people to deal with such feelings. They try to stifle them but often find later that they surface in surprisingly inappropriate ways. The problem is particularly severe for men, who—despite an onslaught of articles telling them it's okay to experience emotions and even to cry—still feel it's unmanly to reveal that they're upset.

Some people find it's helpful to talk to a spouse or close friend about what they're experiencing. Others would rather not share it. But it's important to find a way to let off some of the emotional "steam" constructively. If you're sad and feel like crying, let it rip—in private, if you like (the shower's a wonderful place). If it takes a round of sentimental records, a sappy movie, or a tragic play or novel to move you to tears, indulge. If you're angry, spare the kids and the dog and go punch out a pillow, chop wood for the fireplace, or give the bushes a good pruning.

Sports activities also provide great opportunities for emotional release. Geraldine, the woman mentioned earlier who has learning disabilities, screams as she plays racquetball. Even couch potatoes can let off steam by rooting for their favorite football or basketball team.

And, of course, there's always sex, one of the greatest emotional releases around.

Counseling, Therapy, and Support

Counseling, therapy, and the support of people close to you can all help you manage stress, change the meaning of the situation, or change the situation. Although I have written about them only in this section, they could be included in all the sections on coping. A few examples show how counseling and support help people manage a stressful period.

It was wonderful to see my college roommate, Joan, after thirty-five years. We started talking and joking as if we had never been apart. She quickly caught me up on the good things in her life. She was still married to Bill, whom she had met in college, and they had three fine children. He had done well as an accountant, and she was working as a social worker.

Then she talked at length about the unexpected depression she had just conquered. It had started after a very stressful year, when her mother died, her best friend moved to California, and she stuck by two good friends as they succumbed slowly to cancer. Then her eldest daughter had had a big wedding, which Joan orchestrated.

Joan began to feel depressed after the wedding, and soon depression seemed to consume her. Instead of focusing on all her separations and losses, Joan became obsessed with her husband's close friendship with Sylvia, a friend of hers. She began feeling that her husband paid more attention to Sylvia, even to their dog, than to her. All in all, it was a horrible period; she feared she was going crazy.

I asked Joan what helped her cope. Her immediate answer was, "Friends and a therapist." Her friends assured her that Bill would never stray and that Sylvia flirted with all their husbands. She loved hearing Bill defended and Sylvia criticized.

Her therapist helped her put her losses into perspective and helped her realize that she needed more time to mourn the many changes in her life. She appreciated the therapist's giving her "permission" to be depressed. Together, the comments of friends and her therapist reassured her that she might be overreacting, but she wasn't crazy.

Friends are crucial buffers against stress. But what about the many periods in life when you're alone, due to a move or a change in relationships?

A divorced woman who has recently moved to a new city is clearly having a wonderful time. She made up her mind not to sit home or feel sorry for herself. At first, she often went out to theaters and museums alone. Since she is very sociable and wanted to meet people, she called a local church and found out about their singles discussion groups. Hard as it was, she made herself go. She began talking to the discussion leader, and later he called her for a date. That broke the social ice, and she has been expanding her circle of friends ever since.

Not everyone can go to a singles group. One young man told me that he didn't know how to meet people and that he hated going to bars. His solution was to find the "best" computer dating service in town. Through it, he got the names of three women, and that started off his social life with a bang.

One woman, unemployed and with no prospects for a job, started a self-help club. She promoted a story about the club that had appeared in her local newspaper, which then attracted others to join her club. This activity helped expand her network; it also resulted in part-time work for her, setting up job clubs at a community agency.

One man explains that because he is terribly shy, he cannot do any of the "things" one must do to meet people. He found a good therapist who has helped him explore the underlying reasons for his reluctance to reach out. Over time and with continued therapy, he has begun meeting people and enlarging his social network.

We can see how interrelated counseling and support are. In fact, counseling is sometimes a temporary support for people in transition.

Using Relaxation Skills

Many new techniques such as biofeedback, imaging, and relaxation tapes are designed to help people control their physical reactions to stressful situations. For example, migraine headaches can sometimes be eased through biofeedback. Some claim that imaging—a technique for visualizing clearly in your mind a desired effect—can assist in fighting cancer, and others claim it can produce weight loss.

Relaxation tapes are often used before surgery. One man who had been afraid to admit his fear of surgery was grateful when a friend brought him a tape player and some music cassettes. The friend also slipped in a relaxation tape, which he found very soothing.

Reading

Another strategy for reducing stress is reading, which can both distract and instruct. Self-help books, novels, plays, and advice columns, like Ann Landers, can all help at different times.

When asked to describe a positive transition in his life, one man answered, "I realized I was gay." In describing how he coped with this transition, he explained, "I pretty much handled it by myself. I couldn't turn to my family or friends because I thought they would reject me. . . . I read a lot of material in libraries and in bookstores about homosexuality. I realized through reading that I was like a lot of other people and not simply alone.''

Physical Activity

Jogging, swimming, aerobics, walking, tennis, dancing, and other forms of physical activity have many purposes. They are fun; they drain off excess energy; and they redirect one's concentration away from whatever is worrisome.

The manager of a condominium who was caught in a cross fire of complaints from residents and management says, ''I was going out of my mind.'' Then she started jogging. Both her figure and her mental health improved. She now jogs regularly and feels ''100 percent better.''

For less athletic people, vigorous gardening or housework may do the trick. A woman who took a job in a new city recalls, ''Right after the move I was too embarrassed to admit that I was unhappy. During this period I cleaned house like crazy. The physical activity occupied me until I made a friend.''

Doing Nothing—Deliberate Inaction

One special form of selective ignoring is ''deliberate inaction.'' For many people, the hardest thing is to take no action—to sit tight and wait it out. But sometimes it's a very wise coping move.

I have just finished reading . . . *And Ladies of the Club,* a fascinating chronicle of the late 1800s and early 1900s, woven around a group of leading women in a community who form a club.[11] Anne, the leading character, loves her husband, John, and is shocked that he has occasional liaisons with other women. However, Anne does nothing about her discovery. Why? First, she loves John and knows he loves her. Second, she understands the meaning of these infidelities; they are his way of dealing with a very deep depression. Third, she and John live a very fulfilling life together.

Let me make clear that I am not suggesting that partners should take no action against infidelity. In most cases, that would be very demoralizing. But after wrestling with this issue, Anne concluded that deliberate inaction was the right thing to do in this instance. She did not generally use this strategy; but she used it in this situation for her own reasons.

Taking no action is different from denial. When denying you suppress or delay facing a situation. In deliberate inaction, you are well aware of the situation but consciously decide to do nothing about it.

Using Many Coping *Strategies*

There is no one magic way to cope, but there are many possible strategies to consider and try. In addition to using strategies that change your situation or your way of looking at it, you might: seek out a counselor or therapist; join or start a self-help group; visit special-interest groups or singles groups; take courses; volunteer; try computer dating; start up social activities at work; exercise; read; pray. Some of these probably appeal to you, others clearly don't, and still others are "maybes." The figure 5–1 worksheet

---

Figure 5–1. Your Coping Strategies Worksheet

Possible Coping Strategies	Now Using
• **Taking action to change or modify the transition**	
Negotiating	☐
Taking optimistic action	☐
Seeking advice	☐
Asserting yourself	☐
Brainstorming a new plan	☐
Taking legal action (if needed)	☐

Possible Coping Strategies	Now Using

• Changing the meaning of the transition

Applying knowledge of the transition
  process ☐
Rehearsing ☐
Developing rituals ☐
Making positive comparisons ☐
Rearranging priorities ☐
Relabeling or reframing ☐
Selectively ignoring ☐
Using denial ☐
Using humor ☐
Having faith ☐

• Managing Reactions to Stress

Playing ☐
Using relaxation skills ☐
Expressing emotions ☐
Doing physical activity ☐
Participating in counseling, therapy, or ☐
  support groups
Reading ☐

• Doing nothing

• Other Strategies

_____ ☐
_____ ☐
_____ ☐
_____ ☐

Source: Based on work from L.I. Pearlin and C. Schooler, "The Structure of Coping," *Journal of Health and Social Behavior* 19 (1978): 2–21. Reprinted with permission.

will help enable you to TAKE STOCK of which ones you now use. In the next chapter, as you TAKE CHARGE, you will identify which new ones you might like to try. Remember, it's not the commitment to a particular strategy that makes the difference; it's the commitment to mobilizing your resources, to trying new things, and "hanging in there, baby!" In the next chapter, we'll look more specifically at how to choose the strategies that are best suited to your particular situation.

As one woman who was widowed writes,

> I discovered that I used many coping strategies. Giving in to my sad feelings helped me get through them. I jogged every day, which helped me reduce the stress. I talked to myself, reassuring myself that things would get better and that I could handle the situation. I also talked to trusted others and learned it was more helpful to be listened to than rescued. The emotional pain made the world look gray and bleak, but I felt that the pain lifted, and with it, my spirit, when I was able to have a sense of humor. Although not changing anything, it did provide temporary relief. The process took time; there were many setbacks. I discovered that there is no "best" coping strategy that works in all situations, but no matter how difficult the situation, I will eventually find a way to cope with it.[12]

* * * * *

Your Coping *Strategies* Review

• Do you use a range of strategies?	Yes	No
• Do you sometimes take action to change the transition?	Yes	No
• Do you sometimes try to change the meaning of the transition?	Yes	No
• Do you try to take stress in stride?	Yes	No
• Do you know when to do nothing?	Yes	No

- Do you feel that you can flexibly choose different strategies depending on the challenge at hand?   Yes   No

- Taking all of the above into account, do you rate your *Strategies* as:

A high resource	Yes	No
A low resource	Yes	No
A mixed bag	Yes	No
Okay	Yes	No

TAKING CHARGE

N ow for the $64,000 question: What can you do about your own particular situation?

The third and last section of this book is designed to help you turn your vulnerabilities into strengths and to marshall them in a way that will help you cope with transitions more effectively. Like an athlete preparing for a sports marathon, you *can* develop some skills that will help ensure that your defeats are reversed and that your successes endure. This section focuses on how you can do that.

Chapter 6 raises and answers the question, how do you know which strategies to use? Chapter 7 focuses on an extremely common cluster of transitions—our roles as workers—and demonstrates how you can learn to take charge of them. Chapter 8 addresses the final, most basic question: How can you profit from change?

6

Your Action Plan
for Mastering Change

S OME time ago I delivered a speech on coping to middle managers of a major corporation. After describing the four S's (*Situation, Self, Supports,* and *Strategies*) and the four major categories of coping strategies (taking action to change the transition, changing the meaning of the transition, managing reactions to stress, and choosing to do nothing), I felt I had covered everything anyone needs to know about change. However, the first question proved me wrong. "How do I know when to use a particular strategy?" asked someone from the audience. This challenged me to put together Your Action Plan for Mastering Change.

The Action Plan combines the coping strategies with the four S's to help ease the agonies of change, to neutralize and solve problems, and to turn liabilities into resources. By implementing the steps in sequence, you will see how modifying one or more of the four S's can help you traverse a transition with more creativity and control than otherwise may have seemed possible.

At a recent workshop, one man expressed concern about people who do not think in such systematic ways and who rely more on intuition than on a step-by-step plan. I think his concern is legitimate. I too have often thought that step-by-step plans take the romance and surprise out of living. However, I can think of nothing more romantic than dancing. Yet to dance well and with freedom, one needs to know the steps. Eventually, a good dancer improvises. Similarly, this system of TAKING STOCK and TAKING

CHARGE of change is not meant to hem you in. On the contrary, once you know some basic steps and techniques, you'll be in a position to improvise your own strategies. This chapter provides a framework for empowering you to help yourself. In other words, when you have a knowledge and skill base, you are freed to innovate, experiment, and improvise.

In this chapter I will apply the system to the cases of three people facing transitions: Carolyn, the newlywed who moved to a new city; George, who was laid off by his employer; and Esther, who wanted to end her relationship with her boyfriend.

Then we'll give you a turn to look at your own transition by following the steps to create your own Action Plan for Mastering Change.

These steps are:

- *Step One:* APPROACH CHANGE by identifying the type of transition and the degree to which it has altered your roles, relationships, routines, assumptions.
- *Step Two:* TAKE STOCK of your resources for managing change. First, assess the four S's, which provide a picture of your resources. Focus on the resources you graded ''low'' in order to determine which of the four S's requires strengthening.
- *Step Three:* TAKE CHARGE of the transition by strengthening those resources graded ''low.'' This is your chance to turn the tide by considering which strategy from ''Your Coping *Strategies* Review'' would be most appropriate for shoring up each of the ''low'' resource areas. (When you work on your own plan you may also come up with other strategies that are not on the list.) Then, select a strategy or strategies appropriate for you— ones that have a good chance of success.

The Action Plan cannot definitively solve all of Carolyn, George, Esther's, or your problems. It cannot produce a quick and easy answer, since there is no magic. What it can do is help you analyze your transition systematically and devise one or more strategies for handling the transition in a reassuring, controlled manner.

Carolyn Revisited

When we met Carolyn in chapter 1, she was trying to cope with multiple transitions—a new marriage, a move away from family and church, and a tubular pregnancy. She was APPROACHING a transition that had changed most aspects of her life. As she said, "If you had a ten-point scale and 10 was miserable, I'd be off the scale." The challenge was to help Carolyn figure out what to do about a seemingly endless, miserable forever.

Carolyn's Four S's: TAKING STOCK

Let's begin by filling out Carolyn's Four-S Worksheet (figure 6–1) to rate her coping resources. In assessing her situation, we are reminded that it's important to consider the type of transition, whether or not it is having a major impact on the person's life and the degree to which the person experiencing it feels in control.

Carolyn was facing multiple transitions. Any one of them would have been enough to throw many people for a loop. Cut off from her friends, her relatives, and her church at a time of multiple transitions, she could see immediately that her *situation* offered little more than "low" ratings. Her combination of transitions clearly added up to a "biggie" or double whammy: her new relationship with her husband and the loss of her old stable relationships in her home town; the change imposed on her routine by geographical isolation; the occurrence of the problem pregnancy at a time when she was already under pressure; and her newness both to marriage and to the area where she was living. This resulted in low marks on all her coping resources.

Carolyn's own words, quoted above, show how she felt about her *Self.* She lacked a sense of well-being and self-knowledge and was generally pessimistic.

When we first saw Carolyn, she was sitting at home and crying. She felt bereft of support. Her husband felt that she was withdrawing from him, and he was confused; she was unable to relate to him as an adult. She had never been separated from her family before and blamed her husband for her feelings of isolation. Caro-

---

Figure 6–1 Carolyn Takes Stock

APPROACHING CHANGE

- *Type:* Double Whammy
- *Impact on roles, relationships, routines, assumptions:* Major

TAKING STOCK OF YOUR COPING RESOURCES

Ratings	High	Okay	Low
• *Your Situation:* overall			X
Your evaluation			X
Timing			X
Control			X
Previous experience			X
Other stress			X
• *Your Self:* overall			X
Response to transition (optimist, pessimist)			X
Sense of well-being (mastery and pleasure)			X
Self-knowledge			X
• *Your Supports:* overall			X
Getting affection, affirmation, aid			X
Evaluation—getting enough and the right mixture			X
Interrupted by transition			X
• *Your Coping Strategies:* overall			X
Taking action to change or modify your situation, supports, self, strategies			X
Changing the way you see the transition			X
Managing your reactions to transition			X
Doing nothing			X
Other			X

lyn was simultaneously facing the issues of how to create intimacy with a new husband and how to cope with separation from her family. At the time we first interviewed her, she would have rated her *supports* as low.

Reviewing Carolyn's coping *Strategies,* it became evident that she was using few if any of them. She was "doing nothing"—but not out of choice. She didn't know what to do. She just stayed home feeling overwhelmed.

Carolyn's Action Plan

Carolyn's multiple transitions added up to the serious challenge of low ratings in all four areas. Not only was she facing a very trying series of changes, she was obviously not well equipped to deal with them.

Yet after a year she was able to feel that she had come through the worst, was no longer a complete outsider, and could start to build a satisfying new life. How did this happen?

Although Carolyn could not see how to change her *Situation,* she knew that she needed advice. But she felt too defeated to initiate a search for help. Luckily for Carolyn, one day while she was in the doctor's office the physician's assistant, Molly, noticed how depressed she seemed to be and began to draw her out. When Molly showed empathy with Carolyn's distress about having a pregnancy far away from home, Carolyn began to cry. Molly, trained as a physician's assistant, was taking a graduate degree in social work. She immediately realized how vulnerable Carolyn was and also guessed rightly that Carolyn would not seek help from a professional. Molly suggested that Carolyn come in to talk with her for half an hour before her regular appointments with the doctor. Carolyn did so, and during these sessions she was able to seek Molly's advice about what to do, how to meet people, and how to break out of her depression.

As Carolyn confided in and discussed her *Situation* with the caring, competent Molly, she was able to devise several *Strategies* that eventually helped her turn the tide and get her on the road back to health and optimism.

Figure 6–2 Carolyn Takes Charge

POSSIBLE COPING STRATEGIES	*STRENGTHENING YOUR FOUR S's*
Taking Action to Change or Modify Your Four S's	
Negotiating	Negotiated with husband for use of car and regular long-distance calls to family
Taking optimistic action	Joined church group and new-comers club
Seeking advice	Later started outreach program for others
Asserting yourself	Enrolled in assertiveness training
Brainstorming a new plan	
Taking legal action	
Other	
Changing the Way You See Things	
Applying knowledge of the transition process	Learned that transitions take time and that she could begin to control the outcomes
Developing rituals	
Making positive comparisons	
Rearranging priorities	
Reappraising, relabeling, reframing	From assertiveness training, she learned to feel ''entitled'' to support, car, etc.
Ignoring selectively	

Denying	
Engaging in humor	
Having faith	
Other	
Managing Your Reactions to the Transition	
Playing	Began to socialize with other couples
Using relaxation skills	
Expressing emotions	
Engaging in physical activity	Joined exercise class
Participating in counseling, therapy, or support groups	Became involved in church group, helped work with others who had similar problems of shyness, isolation
Reading	
Other	
Doing Nothing	
Using Other Strategies	

Carolyn's Action Plan (figure 6–2) summarizes what she was able to do. First, she used at least three *Strategies* to change or modify her *Situation:*

Asserting herself. Before she could relate to new friends and begin to make her marriage work, Carolyn needed to change both her *Self* and her coping *Strategies.* With Molly's encouragement, she enrolled in an assertiveness-training group at a nearby church. This helped her learn ways to ask for what she needed without feeling ashamed. Mostly she changed from feeling "unentitled" to feeling "entitled" to support and attention.

Negotiating. Molly encouraged Carolyn to start developing new supports while retaining her connections to her past, so Carolyn negotiated the use of their limited resources with her husband. She suggested to him—and he agreed—that she could use the car twice a week to attend church and that she could spend some of their limited money for long-distance phone calls to her mother three times a week.

Taking optimistic action. When Carolyn first began to participate in activities at the neighborhood church, she was very shy. But with the constant encouragement of her mother (over the phone), she "hung in there." She discovered and joined a newcomers club that really served as a support group. Eventually she and another woman started an outreach program for people too shy to attend the church.

We can see that once you decide to take action on your *Situation,* your decision radiates to action-oriented changes in your *Self,* your *Supports,* and your *Strategies.* Carolyn changed her *Situation* by a combination of seeking advice, negotiating, taking optimistic action, and asserting herself.

Carolyn then began to change the way she sees things. She was helped to understand both her *Situation* and her *Self* differently by reframing. She felt she could not undo the move, the marriage, or the pregnancy, but she was helped to change her perspective and understand why she was so distressed. Previously very critical of herself for her inability to cope, Carolyn was helped through the new support group and counseling to understand and accept the difficulty of coping with transitions that seem beyond one's control. Clearly she had been involved in the decision to marry, but she had not been in control of the move or tubular pregnancy.

Just knowing that many people naturally are upset when they feel they are out of control can help. But even more important, Molly helped Carolyn realize that she was not a puppet and that she could learn to control her reactions and become more of an optimist. At first, Carolyn did not believe these new words, but as time passed she began to believe that she could, in fact, gain control over her life.

By acquiring knowledge about the transition process, Carolyn was helped to change the way she viewed her *Situation.* She came to understand several major characteristics of transitions and thus enhanced her ability to flow with them.

Many people ask, "How long will it take to resolve my transition?" Unfortunately, no formula can accurately predict the answer to that question. Some authors outline a specific series of stages that everyone experiences as they go through transitions, but I do not believe that life is that clear-cut. My own research shows that the particular phases and their corresponding lengths of time vary greatly depending on how long it takes one to reshape a new and satisfying life: a new set of roles, relationships, routines, and assumptions.

At first Carolyn felt betwixt and between her new and old roles and routines, and she had no notion that she could become comfortable in her new ones. But she learned that people shifting from one role (such as from single person to married one) pass through three phases: first, identification with the old role; second, leaving the old role but not yet knowing how to behave in the new one; and third, finally, comfort in the new role.

Carolyn also took steps to manage better her reactions to the transition. She joined a support group in the church, continued to see Molly for three months, and joined an exercise class. She began to have a little fun and relaxation. She even met some people and initiated a social event with spouses.

Carolyn's experience demonstrates that using the Four-S system makes it possible to progress from a feeling of helplessness and defeat to feelings of optimism and hope, thereby transforming trauma into a significant, positive change in one's life.

George, the Man Who Was Riffed

George was working in a large corporation when the word came down that due to financial losses, there would be a RIF (reduction in force) and 5 percent of the staff would lose employment. "I knew my job was not in jeopardy,'' he told me. ''The RIF had been explained, and our department was exempt. So the day my boss told me we had a meeting with his boss, I was excited, certain I was going to get a new challenge. But at that meeting my boss's boss told me that the RIF *would* affect my job: I would have to leave in six weeks!

''I couldn't make myself talk. I couldn't even make my legs move so I could get out the door. I just sat there, stunned. As I look back at that moment, I can now understand why I was so immobilized. Not long before, my wife had left me for another person and my father had moved in with me after he was diagnosed as having terminal cancer. And here they were telling me I'd lose my job! Not only would I be out of work, but I'd be cut off from the company's theater group—the center of my social and recreational life.''

What was it about George's *Situation* that made him so vulnerable? How could George be helped to turn the tide?

George's Four S's: TAKING STOCK

When we TAKE STOCK of George's resources for coping at this particular time, we can readily see why he was too upset to get himself to the car (figure 6–3).

As George APPROACHED this transition, he saw his *Situation*—the RIF—as out of his control, as very negative and permanent. In addition, he had many other stresses. The recent departure of his wife for another man and his father's coming to live with him had already taken their toll. The prospect of losing his leisure and social life as well as his job was overwhelming. So we see a transition in which George would rate his *Situation* as ''low.'' But despite his multiple losses (wife, colleagues on the job, theater group), he still had a few close friends. In addition, his father became a support as well as a drain since he was at home, able to encourage him and help him weather the storm. Also, George felt he mattered to his father, and that made George feel useful. So his *Supports* were mixed, but mostly low.

Figure 6–3   George Takes Stock

APPROACHING CHANGE

- *Type:* Surprise
- *Impact on roles, relationships, routines, assumptions:* Major

TAKING STOCK OF YOUR COPING RESOURCES

Ratings	High	Okay	Low
• *Your Situation:* overall			X
Your evaluation			X
Timing			X
Control		X	
Previous experience			X
Other stress			X
• *Your Self:* overall		X	
Response to transition (optimist, pessimist)			X
Sense of well-being (mastery and pleasure)		X	
Self-knowledge	X		
• *Your Supports:* overall			X
Getting affection, affirmation, aid		X	
Evaluation—getting enough and the right mixture		X	
Interrupted by transition			X
• *Your Coping Strategies:* Overall		X	
Taking action to change or modify your situation, supports, self, strategies		X	
Changing the way you see the transition	X		
Managing your reactions to transition			X
Doing nothing			
Other			

He usually saw his *Self* as optimistic, and he used a variety of coping *Strategies*. During our interview (the week of the RIF) George repeatedly contrasted the positive way he had always seen himself—as a coper—with his current evaluation, saying, "I feel like a loser." We rated his *Self* as "okay," though he clearly felt low at that moment.

George kept saying, "I don't know what to do. I don't know how to cope." But what gave George a handle on his transition was the fact that he continually referred to how he used to be a good coper. As he said, "I always was the one to tell my friends how to cope. Now I'm stuck." The fact that he had coped in the past but couldn't cope now made us feel he would be able to use his strategies again. We therefore marked *Strategies* as "okay." The combination of personal, social, and professional blows caused a crisis of confidence.

He would therefore rate his *Situation* as low, his *Self* as okay, his *Supports* as low, and his *Strategies* as okay.

George's Action Plan

After identifying his weak resources, George turned to his Action Plan (figure 6–4) and worked his way through his possible coping *Strategies*.

His first task was to figure out how to change his *Situation* and his *Supports,* which were both low.

"Do I *want* to take action?" he asked himself. "And if so, what can I do?"

Second, George asked himself whether he wanted to change the way he viewed his *Situation* or his *Supports,* and whether he could benefit from managing his reactions to the transition. Finally, he considered the option of doing nothing or of devising other methods of coping.

Here's what George did:

Managing his reactions: Because George was so distressed, he first focused on strategies for managing his reactions so that he could feel calmer and more in control. He began by enrolling in a support program instituted by his employer to assist RIFFED employees in obtaining new jobs. At the end of a week-long seminar, George had a résumé, a plan for securing a new job, and a "buddy" from the personnel office to help him identify job leads. He also had a better understanding of the psychological aspects of the RIF experience—that leaving a job involves mourning, as when leaving a loved one. George also sought and received personal counseling that helped him manage his stress. He stopped blaming himself for his failed marriage and stopped seeing himself as a victim. At the end of six weeks, George had accepted a new job with a new organization and was making even more money than before.

Taking action to change his situation and supports: George realized that one of his biggest losses was no longer being able to participate in the theater group at work. After the shock began to wear off and he began to get his bearings, he spoke to the director from the company theater group, who personally arranged for George to become involved with a community theater group. They agreed that George would work with the set designers on the next show. Once that was arranged, George felt much better about his entire situation.

Changing the way he saw the transition: George felt very defeated after his wife left him. He kept blaming himself and thinking he must be no good. He was not able to let go of those feelings, but after reading self-help books and talking with friends and a counselor, he began to see that it would take time to get over the failed marriage and his feelings of rejection. George realized that with therapy he might be able to sort out what roles he and his wife had played in the breakup of the marriage and what he might be able to do differently in future relationships. He was nowhere near that resolution, but he began to see that he could, with work, get there. George began to say that if he could survive the double loss of wife and job, he could handle anything. Quite apart from his work and recreational problems, George faced another problem. He felt imposed upon by his father. But this matter came into perspective after he saw a television show in which a young man places his father in a nursing home and ends up feeling very guilty. This show helped George realize that his caring for his father had helped distract him from his own problems and had helped him maintain a good view of himself.

Figure 6–4   George Takes Charge

POSSIBLE COPING STRATEGIES	STRENGTHENING YOUR FOUR S's
Taking Action to Change or Modify Your Four S's	
Negotiating	
Taking optimistic action	
Seeking advice	Sought advice from theater director who arranged for him to work in similar group
Asserting yourself	
Brainstorming a new plan	
Taking legal action	
Other	
Changing the Way You See Things	
Applying knowledge of the transition process	
Developing rituals	
Making positive comparisons	
Rearranging priorities	
Reappraising, relabeling, reframing	Realized that miserable as he was about the breakup of his marriage, he had an opportunity to learn about himself so that the same mistakes would not be made again
Ignoring selectively	

Denying

Engaging in humor

Having faith

Other

**Managing Your
Reactions to the
Transition**

Playing

Using relaxation skills

Expressing emotions

Engaging in physical
  activity

Participating in coun-
  seling, therapy, or
  support groups
	Participated in outplacement coun-
	seling sponsored by employer and
	after several weeks found another
	job. Found counselor and began
	exploring how to cope with transi-
	tions, feelings of failure, and the
	pain of rejection

Reading

Other

Doing Nothing

**Using Other
Strategies**

Breaking Up:
Esther's Story in Her Own Words

"Leaving a marriage or relationship that is bad for you—or, as is more often the case, *not good* for you—is one of the most difficult of all transitions to make. For me, the transition was to stop going with Barry, to end our two-year exclusive relationship, and to stop spending most of my time with him. I wanted to meet someone with whom I could share my life more fully. It took me a long time to carry out my decision, and sometimes I wavered. Although it was a change I wanted, it was scary. I felt the terror most strongly when I awoke in the morning filled with anxiety about the prospect of being out there, of not having a man in my life (especially when my brother had just started a new romance), of being alone, and worse, of being lonely. But if such reasons were to become the glue of my relationship with Barry, I knew it had better be dismantled.

"I cannot tell you how much the Four-S System helped me make this change. I will not try to present it here in logical progression, or even explain what it is. But I will tell, in bits and pieces, how its essential wisdom influenced my decisions and helped me carry them out *now,* instead of months from now or perhaps never.

"I was aware that it was five painful days before Valentine's Day. How could I live through Valentine's Day thinking as I was and saying nothing? I decided to analyze my potential transition according to the Four-S System. I first looked at my possible *Situation.* It is terrifying to end a relationship. People will more readily quit their jobs, part with their money, and give up old friends and even their children than end a bad relationship. (How many people live in quiet desperation with the wrong person because they believe there's nobody else out there?) Striking out alone seemed less terrifying when I considered that I had been through breakups before. True, I had not initiated them. But I remember being relieved when they ended and *never* wanting—when an 'ex' had second thoughts and wanted to get together again—to resume.

"Next, I looked at my *Supports* and external resources: I could tick them off. I liked my job. The first half of a new book I had written had been accepted with enthusiasm. I would soon pay off a ten-year debt to my former husband. I had many friends who are stable and supportive and a church that was a joy to attend. They even sell my other three books at the Book Nook each Sunday, where I am asked often to autograph a copy.

"Finally, I knew without enumerating that my inner resources—my *Self*—were stronger than they had ever been before. After six years of psychotherapy, my habit of negative thinking had been broken, and I no longer felt depressed or unsure of myself. My life was going in the direction I wanted: I had just passed my annual physical, I was working out four to five times a week, and I even had prospects of fitting into a size 10 bathing suit by summer. I had fulfilled the prophecy of a man I met years ago: 'You will really hit your pace when you reach your early forties.'

"Some odd thoughts popped into my mind. I had a new car that wasn't, like the old one, breaking down every month or so. I knew how to fix, or pay someone to fix, most of the things that broke down in my house. I knew where to find college students to do yard work and other jobs.

"As I understand the Four-S System, you count your pluses in four areas: your *Situation, Self, Supports,* and *Strategies.* You also look for weak spots that can be strengthened. The timing was not good. I would be losing not only a lover but a roommate. I could look for a new roommate, but I had no time to look, nor to deal with the distractions roommates invariably present. As for sex and male companionship, there would be little time for that while I had a book to finish.

"I had never fully overcome a deep sense of dependency and need to always have a man in my life. I feared that losing the security of this relationship would keep me from concentrating fully on my book. Could I stay home alone nights writing, knowing nobody would be coming over later to spend the night? Should I wait and break off with Barry *after* my book was finished?

"Questions helped me identify my strengths and weaknesses. The question remained not Should I? but Can I?

"I decided to do it. On a Sunday afternoon before Valentine's Day, I invited Barry over for a cup of tea (my beverage of choice in a crisis) and told him, 'I want always to be friends with you, but I do not want to continue the relationship we have had.'

"I was ending it because I believed I could have an even better life in the future. I was ending it because I would have a chance to cage the dragon of my dependency. I was ending it because I believe you have to say good-bye before you can say hello.''

Esther's Four S's: TAKING STOCK

As Esther thought about her ability to cope, she realized that over the years she had learned when to take action and when to sit tight and do nothing. She carried out a consistent but sensible exercise regime, went to church regularly, and pretty much knew what was going on, as she put it, ''inside myself.''

Esther assessed her *Situation,* her *Self,* her *Supports,* and her *Strategies* and decided to initiate a change in her relationship with Barry. Her *Situation* for leaving was not ideal because of her work deadline, but it was definitely within her control, so we will give it an overall rating of ''okay'' (see figure 6–5). In terms of her *Self,* Esther had entered psychotherapy, was feeling much better about herself as a person, and saw herself in a positive light. She was also aware that she had great dependency needs that influenced her to attach herself and stick to a man. Her overall rating of *Self* is ''high.'' She discussed her many supportive friends and her church, making a ''high'' for *Supports.* She also felt she was able to utilize many *Strategies,* making that another ''high'' resource.

To summarize: Esther's resources for coping with change were mostly high. By TAKING STOCK of these, she realized she was ready for change, that if she was going to make it, this would be the time to do it. However, she also realized two areas of vulnerability: the timing and her possible dependency needs, which surfaced as a need to always have a ''man to rely on.''

Esther's Action Plan

Even though Esther's resources outweighed her deficits, she realized that the loss she was initiating would be difficult. She therefore decided to prevent any disasters by actively using many *Strategies* (figure 6–6).

Figure 6–5 Esther Takes Stock

APPROACHING CHANGE

- *Type:* Elected
- *Impact on roles, relationships, routines, assumptions:* Medium

TAKING STOCK OF YOUR COPING RESOURCES

Ratings	High	Okay	Low
• *Your Situation:* overall		X	
Your evaluation		X	
Timing		X	
Control			X
Previous experience		X	
Other stress		X	
• *Your Self:* overall	X		
Response to transition (optimist, pessimist)	X		
Sense of well-being (mastery and pleasure)	X		
Self-knowledge	X		
• *Your Supports:* overall	X		
Getting affection, affirmation, aid	X		
Evaluation—getting enough and the right mixture		X	
Interrupted by transition		X	
• *Your Coping Strategies:* overall	X		
Taking action to change or modify your situation, supports, self, strategies			
Changing the way you see the transition			
Managing your reactions to transition			
Doing nothing			
Other			

Figure 6–6   Esther Takes Charge

POSSIBLE COPING STRATEGIES	*STRENGTHENING YOUR FOUR S's*
Taking Action to Change or Modify Your Four S's	
Negotiating	
Taking optimistic action	Decided to make a break with full awareness of her dependency needs
Seeking advice	
Asserting yourself	
Brainstorming a new plan	
Taking legal action	
Other	
Changing the Way You See Things	
Applying knowledge of the transition process	Awareness of ups and downs that are part and parcel of transitions
Developing rituals	
Making positive comparisons	
Rearranging priorities	
Reappraising, relabeling, reframing	
Ignoring selectively	
Denying	
Engaging in humor	
Having faith	
Other	

Managing Your Reactions to the Transition	
Playing	
Using relaxation skills	Read books about breakups and losses
Expressing emotions	
Engaging in physical activity	Joined hiking club/kept up exercise
Participating in counseling, therapy, or support groups	Became very active in church discussion group
Reading	Read books related to loss
Other	
Doing Nothing	
Using Other Strategies	Wrote her own story as a way to think it through

First, she took optimistic action and decided to make the break with full awareness of her dependency needs. Then she spent a great deal of energy managing her reactions to the transition. Esther selected a strategy uniquely suited to her—writing. She wrote up her own story in terms of the transition model. This process of writing was therapeutic and reinforced her decision to stick with the breakup. She read books about breakups and losses, keeping in mind the wisdom expressed in Judith Viorst's *Necessary Losses,* that there is no way to live a life without facing loss.[1] Esther also made sure she was involved with supportive friends by regularly attending church and participating in the weekly discussion group for singles. Esther also had a fallback plan: if she felt her dependency needs getting out of hand, she would revisit her therapist.

Esther's case illustrates the importance of planning, even when you initiate a change.

It's Your Turn Now

In this chapter I have shared the experiences of three different people who faced different types of transitions and have tried to understand how the system—APPROACHING, TAKING STOCK, and TAKING CHARGE—helped them to cope and manage these changes. Now it's time to apply the system to your own transition or transitions. To help you develop your own Action Plan, follow the steps outlined in this chapter.

First, APPROACH your transition by identifying its type and indicating the degree to which it would alter your life. Second, TAKE STOCK by filling out Your Four-S Worksheet (figure 6–7). This will give you an assessment of where your strengths are and help you identify areas to work on.

Then TAKE CHARGE by filling out Your Action Plan (figure 6–8). You will visually see the resources that need help—your *Situation, Self, Supports,* and *Strategies.* You can then examine your list of possible coping *Strategies* and ask yourself the following series of questions:

- Should you take action to change the S's that are low? If so, which of the *Strategies* could you use?
- Should you try to change the way you see the *S* that needs help? If so, which of the *Strategies* seems most appropriate?
- Should you try to manage your reactions to the transition by reading, praying, jogging, or going into therapy?
- Or should you do nothing?

Again, remember that there may be other strategies that you would find helpful that are not mentioned in this book.

Before you fill out your worksheets, remember these important facts about transitions:

- Change in your life can come from nonevents as well as from events. What is important is the degree to which the event or nonevent alters your life.

Figure 6–7 You Take Stock

APPROACHING CHANGE

- *Type:* _____

- *Impact on roles, relationships, routines, assumptions:* _____

TAKING STOCK OF YOUR COPING RESOURCES

Ratings   *High Okay Low*

- *Your Situation:* overall

  Your evaluation
  Timing
  Control
  Previous experience
  Other stress

- *Your Self:* overall

  Response to transition (optimist, pessimist
  Sense of well-being (mastery and pleasure)
  Self-knowledge

- *Your Supports:* overall

  Getting affection, affirmation, aid
  Evaluation—getting enough and the right mixture
  Interrupted by transition

- *Your Coping Strategies:* overall

  Taking action to change or modify your situation, supports, self, strategies
  Changing the way you see the transition
  Managing your reactions to transition
  Doing nothing
  Other

Figure 6–8 You Take Charge

POSSIBLE COPING STRATEGIES	*STRENGTHENING YOUR FOUR S's*
Taking Action to Change or Modify Your Four S's	
Negotiating	
Taking optimistic action	
Seeking advice	
Asserting yourself	
Brainstorming a new plan	
Taking legal action	
Other	
Changing the Way You See Things	
Applying knowledge of the transition process	
Developing rituals	
Making positive comparisons	
Rearranging priorities	
Reappraising, relabeling, reframing	
Ignoring selectively	
Denying	
Engaging in humor	
Having faith	
Other	

**Managing Your
Reactions to the
Transition**

Playing

Using relaxation
  skills

Expressing emotions
Engaging in physical
  activity

Participating in coun-
  seling, therapy, or
  support groups

Reading

Other

Doing Nothing

**Using Other
Strategies**

• TAKING STOCK of your resources to cope with a particular
transition or set of transitions is based on the assumption that
your resources for coping—your four S's—are not static but will
and can shift throughout your life.

Let me explain. After moving seventeen times, one woman
said, "I have finally had it. No more." What had changed? Her
husband, a career State Department official, had told her when
they married to expect lots of moves. She did. They did. She saw
herself as someone who could pick up, leave, and then dig in new
roots. She was an optimist, used lots of coping strategies, and was
able to develop new supports quickly. She was "high" on her four
S's. But before the seventeenth move, she learned that she had
cancer. She felt vulnerable and unable to just go and start over

again. She did not feel she had the energy to make connections for herself and her young teenagers. In other words, her *Situation* had changed from high to low, influencing her evaluation of her ability to cope.

Someone else, another young woman who had been afraid to move, began to feel that she could move and travel. After several years of therapy, she realized that her fear had been based on anxiety about separating from everything familiar. She now realized her live-in would still be there for her, and her parents would still be there. In her case the biggest shift was in her *Self.*

Any of your four S's might, can, and will change. As they change, your ability to tackle transitions also changes. The encouraging aspect of this model is the knowledge that everything is not preordained. If you feel like a ''loser,'' that can shift. If you feel you've got it together, that's great as long as you realize your *Situation, Self, Supports,* and *Strategies* might and can change.

Because your resources can and do shift, you can employ different strategies to TAKE CHARGE, depending on which resources need strengthening.

As you can see, your coping resources are not precise or scientifically measurable because to some degree they grow out of gut feelings and intuition. Don't be afraid to use these feelings along with the information from the chart to assess your *Situation,* your *Self,* your *Supports,* and your *Strategies.* With these tools you can determine where your vulnerabilities are; you can decide whether to move ahead and how.

These worksheets, your intuition, and your good sense are your guidelines for mastering change. Only you can decide whether and how to implement them. To encourage those who are feeling skeptical or overwhelmed, I want to conclude by saying that I am continually impressed with the creativity of those in transition who devise new ways to cope with and ultimately master and manage change.

7

TAKING CHARGE of Your Work Transitions

W ORK is a core experience in the life of almost every adult. Its undeniable importance is demonstrated by the fact that most of us spend about half our waking hours for the major part of our lives engaged in work. But work is too significant to be defined only in terms of the time spent on it, because where we work, the type of work we do, what we get paid for it, how we relate to other workers, and work's impact on our personal and family lives all play a major role in defining our role in society. Work, in all its facets, dominates a major part of the life of most people.

Furthermore, the pace of technological change has made the workplace and our work lives into a hotbed of transitions. In his chapter I will demonstrate how we can apply what we have learned about transitions to this critically important area of our lives.

The decision to focus on work transitions in this chapter does not imply that other aspects of life—family, community, religion, self development—are less important. I selected one area simply to illustrate the usefulness of applying the steps described in this book to any aspect of living.

To do that, we will follow the system described in the Introduction. We will follow the road map for managing any change, which includes APPROACHING CHANGE, TAKING STOCK OF CHANGE, and TAKING CHARGE OF CHANGE. First, we will look at work transitions in terms of how we APPROACH them; then we will TAKE STOCK of our resources to cope with work; and we will then review how we might TAKE CHARGE of our work transitions.

APPROACHING Work Transitions

Your approach to change will be easier once you have a basic understanding of what transitions are, what the transition process is, and the different types of impacts that transitions can have on your life. Every transition does not alter your life in the same way. Some are big and alter all aspects of your life; others only change one aspect. Furthermore, transitions do not occur at only one point in time. Rather, they are a process that reveals itself over time. Your reactions and emotions change from the beginning of that process to the time when you finally integrate the change into your life.

This knowledge can help you in two ways. First, just knowing that today is not forever, that your reactions will change over time, that only you know if a transition is a major one, can be a comfort. However, you will see that you need different kinds of support and help depending on where you are in the transition process. Let's play this out for work transitions and see if this knowledge can help you approach your next work transition more effectively.

If we look at work transitions as a process over time, we can place them in one of three categories: moving in, moving through, and moving out. Your reactions as you move into a new job will differ from your reactions as you move through or out. In addition, the strategies you employ to smooth the transitions will differ depending on whether you are moving in, through, or out.

Moving In: "Learning the Ropes"

I remember my first job as a camp counselor, then what I called my first "real" job as a secretary to a dean, then my first "real, real" job as a director of admissions of a trade school, then my first "professional" job as a professor, then my change of jobs as a professor to another university. All these experiences involved moving into new roles. I needed help in orienting myself to the new job and new setting.

Whenever you take a new job, whether it is a first job, a new job at the same level (called a lateral move), or a promotion, you need to "learn the ropes." One man reported his confusion when on the first day of his job as administrative assistant his boss announced that "we have several meetings today." When the boss got ready to go to the first meeting, the administrative assistant also prepared to attend. The boss quickly explained that the assistant was not to join him. In this case the new employee needed to get used to the language of the boss—that *we* really meant *I.*

In a similar case, the new vice president of a company was unaware of the informal expectation that all executives would eat in the executive dining room at a particular time. She kept making lunch dates with people she knew in other organizations. Some time passed before she realized that her lack of knowledge about the informal norms had been responsible for excluding her from the inner circle. In another case a man reported his surprise when he learned the unwritten rule that he was expected to raise money to support his salary and his office—a matter that had never been mentioned during the job interviews and orientation. And most recently, I received a letter from a woman executive who had tracked her first day on a temporary assignment with an agency. She wrote:

"I felt a little like a school girl going back to school after a summer vacation. I felt excited about the possibilities. I knew what to expect in general, but the specifics of a new class, and a new teacher were unknown. When I arrived, there was no formal welcoming but I have had enough jobs to know how to take care of myself. I quickly identified the person who could be the biggest help, the secretary to the head of the department. By allying with her, I realized that I would learn the rules and procedures. She made me feel at home."

Meryl Louis suggests that all newcomers to the workplace are in for change and surprise about what is expected.[1] She suggests that turnover and stress occur because of unrealistic, inflated, and unmet expectations. Your transition can be eased, however, by realizing that *any* job will probably evoke feelings of uncertainty and that each time you move into a new setting you will need to learn the ropes. Then you can seek help from an "informal socializing agent," a colleague who can help you understand the procedures and expectations in your new employment. Many employers now designate a partner for each newcomer for this purpose, but if yours does not, you can identify someone as your "partner" to help you understand the culture of the organization, what is expected of you, and how to learn the informal norms. Just knowing that adjusting to transitions takes time and that your reactions will change as you are in the job will be some comfort.

Some of us don't move into a job without a struggle. Unemployed persons often require special supports and strategies. One man who had been unemployed for two years described his period of unemployment as a roller coaster. At first he had been excited about the challenge of finding a new job, then he became discouraged, and eventually he became depressed. He especially hated the way he was treated when he went to parent-teacher meetings. Invariably comments were made about his taking over the role of "mother." Because his wife worked to support the family, and because he, himself, believed that a man's role was to support his family, he felt humiliated.

Two women, while both were out of work, wrote an instructive book called *When Smart People Fail.* The book describes ways to turn this period (which may seem to go on forever) into a productive experience.[2] Even more important than the specific strategies suggested in the book is the public recognition that many are in the same boat.

One strategy that has helped some people who are out of work is the "job club." Once an unemployed person is enrolled in a job club, the enrollee begins to treat the process of looking for a job itself as a job. Enrolled individuals go to club headquarters daily, engage in specific activities with a leader, and participate in group support sessions. The participants learn not to blame themselves and to use job-finding skills in a systematic fashion. Many people don't know where to find job clubs, and many communities don't have them. However, individuals in these communities can incorporate their principles and find an out-of-work partner to work on specific job-seeking strategies; the process makes them feel less alone.

As a result of a reduction in the work force in a federal agency, one policy analyst lost her job. She began pounding the pavement looking for a new job but found nothing. She applied for a number of jobs and sometimes didn't even get an acknowledgment of her application. At other times she was interviewed but not hired. As time passed, she began to doubt her own competence and had nightmares about going on welfare. She finally put an ad in the daily paper announcing a support group for women out of work. Five people answered the ad, and a support group was formed. During the year of meetings the group members defined their career needs, explored their career goals, and developed strategies to reach their goals. One woman borrowed money and opened a bookstore; another woman returned to social work school; another entered a retail trainee program; and one went to work as a temporary secretary and began taking ceramics courses seriously.

Both men and women find unemployment an especially stressful time. Although the lack of financial security is, of course, the number-one issue, the men and women I have interviewed also report negative psychological effects, feeling like a ''nobody,'' when they are out of work.

Turning frustration and despair around is not easy. Getting through this period is less trying if you can get some extra doses of support. Some techniques include informational interviews with people in fields of interest. Such encounters can lead to informal mentoring, brainstorming, counseling, or even jobs. I often suggest that those looking for work consider volunteering one day a week with a person or organization that is relevant to their interests. By making yourself invaluable, you might create a job for yourself.

Moving Through

If the motto for those moving *in* is ''learn the ropes,'' the motto for those moving *through* could be ''hang in there, baby!'' After working in the same job for some time, many of us begin to lose enthusiasm for it. Sometimes this surfaces as "burnout"; at other times it surfaces as a feeling that your are "plateaued" or stuck in the same job with no possibility of change. The questions are: how to sustain your energy and commitment for however long you are in a particular job; what you can do to "hang in there"; and how you know when to leave.

Judith Bardwick suggests that bored employees confront three types of plateaus: structural, content, and life. *Structural* plateaus occur when an employee has no place to go in the organization itself, no new job possibilities, because of the structure of the organization. As an example, Bardwick describes IBM, which at that time employed 383,000 employees, 44,000 managers, 6,000 middle managers, 1,400 executives, and 50 core leaders.[3] Clearly, only a very small proportion could continue to move up.

Of course, not everyone wants to move up. Many people are challenged by the work at hand, while others are unhappy doing the same work. I asked a clerical worker what she would do if there were no obstacles, and she answered, "Just what I am doing." Yet many clerical workers are plateaued. In fact, clerical work is seen as a highly stressful occupation with high demand and low control. That is, workers are under enormous pressure and have little control over what they do and when.

However, many workers are bored because of job content; they have been doing the same job for a number of years. They know what to expect every day. The value of sabbaticals, academics' chance to get away and retool, has been recognized by several other professions. But most professionals and blue-collar workers don't have the luxury of taking a breather. For those who have some discretionary time in their jobs, boredom can be alleviated by assigning new activities while retaining the same jobs. For example, one personnel-department employee had been doing the same job for fifteen years. She found out that her company had a tuition reimbursement plan and entered a graduate program in counseling. As a result of taking courses, she instituted a planning seminar for the firm's employees who were considering retirement. This added a new twist to what the organization regularly did. This enterprising employee had the same job and the same title but was engaging in new activities that energized her.

If you are fortunate enough to work in an organization that has a policy that encourages worker participation, you are less likely to be bored. According to many studies, workers consulted about how to improve their jobs and how to work cooperatively become more involved and productive. Unfortunately, most people don't work in such forward-thinking organizations and need to redesign their jobs in other ways. One domestic worker does this by only accepting jobs in homes where she is encouraged to clean the house as she thinks best. She reports that many employers want to tell her what to do and when. She is good at her work and will not work in homes where all control is taken from her.

A mid-life man working as an engineer fits into what Bardwick labels a *plateau* because of "life." He summarizes his frustrating situation this way:

> I don't know what I am going to say to you. I just got this feeling that I'm kind of just dead-end. I got a job, it's all right, but there is no future. And I see younger men getting ahead of me. Here I have a house, a mortgage. I don't have the freedom to move as they do, but yet I get passed over for promotions. I got a good job, but it is going nowhere; it's just absolutely becoming part of my life that I don't like. I come to work, I do my job, I go home—there's no challenge. . . . If only I saw someplace I could move, someplace I could go, someplace I could get ahead, do some of the things I really wanted to so when I started in this organization. . . . The kids are getting older, I'm becoming less necessary there. You look at this organization—I'm becoming less necessary here. I've got a lot to offer. I just don't know what to do with it.

This man was bored with life; he was experiencing a nonevent. His daily routines were not changing, but something more basic *was* changing: the way he saw himself. He was beginning to see himself as a loser, as nonessential, as a person with no future. His roles and relationships changed when an employee who had previously worked for him became his supervisor. Many plateaued employees are experiencing nonevents, but they lack the support that comes when transitions are more observable.

Moving Out

One student in my class on transitions had just left the Peace Corps. She had enrolled in the class not so much for its academic content but in the hope that it would help her better understand and handle her own transition. She reported that as a volunteer she received extensive orientation, both to the country she would work in and to the overall norms and expectations of the Peace Corps. During her tenure she had had support from other volunteers and had never felt burned out. But now that she had left she felt purposeless and depressed. The contrast of going from an environment in which she had felt she really mattered, was appreciated, and noticed to one in which she was just an individual left her feeling "rudderless." She had no help in coping with this leaving process and was confused about how to proceed.

The process of writing a paper about a proposed workshop for Peace Corps volunteers leaving the program was therapeutic. Apparently this volunteer's problem was shared by many others, and the Peace Corps is now experimenting with different offerings to assist volunteers as they leave and reenter their lives back home.

M.R. Louis writes about what she calls the "leave-taking process," noting that it "can be compared to closing out ledger books account by account, but without knowing until the process is actually occurring what the titles of the accounts . . . will be."[4]

Whether you are fired or leave a job for a promotion, there is bound to be disruption in your life. One woman who voluntarily left one college presidency for another said, "My biggest surprise was depression. I had loved being at my former institution, but felt it was time to leave. I accepted a job at a more complex institution and was very excited about the new job. I expected sadness about leaving so many friends and colleagues. What I did not expect was the pain to continue. I have been gone for six months, and I still cry easily."

College graduates, whose "work" for years has been studying, may experience some of the same problems of moving out as those leaving the work force.

One writer on transitions suggests that once one set of goals is reached, there is an inevitable letdown until a new sense of purpose can be articulated. The learners moving out are giving up classes, advisers, and the goal of "becoming," but they may not yet have moved to a new set of activities and self-definition. Change involves loss as well as gain in what one writer calls "the articulation of ambivalence."[5] Grief is often the reponse to leaving one set of activities, even when the change is one that is desired, like finishing a degree or accepting a promotion. There are contradictory impulses—a yearning for the past and a drive to formulate new agendas.

To summarize: We have approached work transitions by looking at them as a process over time. All through your life you will undergo many work transitions. You will move into many new situations requiring that you "learn the ropes." You will also find yourself remaining in job situations where you need to develop strategies that will enable you to "hang in there." Many times you will leave a job where your task is to "let go and reinvest." There will also be times when you are trying to get in or out of the labor market, where you need help to "stay the course." This knowledge base will give you the perspective needed to master your work transitions.

TAKING STOCK of Your Four S's

Your knowledge of coping with transitions provides you with a framework for thinking about how best to help yourself, depending on whether you are moving in, moving through, or moving out of work. Now we go to the next part of the transition system— TAKING STOCK of your potential resources for managing your work transitions. Here we will look at your four S's—your overall *Situation,* your *Self,* your *Supports,* and your *Strategies* for coping.

Let's look at the experience of Helen, who is a building engineer, as she moved into, through, out of, and then into two different jobs. In both cases, her primary work responsibilities involved fixing leaks in a building, checking out electrical problems, confirming that the heat and air conditioning were working properly, and being on call to address any emergencies.

She took the first job several years ago, in an office building, and after six months she left it. In order to understand what happened, let's TAKE STOCK of Helen's four S's. At the time she took the job she was in a trying *Situation*. She had just left her husband and had total responsibility for three small children. The combination of job and personal changes were very stressful. Helen began to blame herself for not being able to make a go of her marriage and began thinking globally about her *Self* as a failure. She had some *Supports* among family members, but at work there was little support and little control over what she did. She punched a clock and followed the rules, but never was told she was doing a good job. She spent most of the time in the boiler room and had little contact with anyone at work. Helen's greatest resource was her willingness to try many *Strategies* at home and at work. Overall she had three "low" S's and one "high" S—not enough to make her able to "move in" easily.

More recently, Helen took a similar job in another office building. She is now living with a partner with whom she is very compatible. He is very involved with the children and very committed to her well-being. She sees her *Situation* as excellent. Although she still tends to downplay her own capabilities, Helen is now aware of her tendencies to see the glass as half empty rather than half full. Her *Support* at home and work is now "high." Her boss at work is very appreciative of her performance and keeps saying how lucky he is to have her on his staff. Her coping *Strategies* are good; she is able to be assertive when necessary, to hold back when appropriate, and to think differently at times.

Work-related transitions, whether we are employed or unemployed, have certain characteristics and phases in common. Yet as Helen's story shows, what we bring to the transition at a particular time of life may determine to a large extent whether we master it. TAKING STOCK of your four S's will enable you to identify the areas you need to bolster to help you cope with the transition: your *Situation,* your *Self,* your *Supports,* or your *Strategies.*

TAKING CHARGE of Your Four S's

Once you have TAKEN STOCK of your four S's, the next step is to TAKE CHARGE of them. This means taking control, influencing the course of events or your relationships with people.

John is a young man who was in a partnership with two others in restoring an old farm that they hoped to sell. The partners began to disagree about how much each was doing. They began to think of dissolving the partnership. However, John argued that he had already invested a considerable amount of time and money in the project and had given up other work opportunities. How could he regain control?

John found that he could APPROACH this work transition as a learning experience and that it was not necessary to make a long-term commitment to it. This helped him view the experience as important for "learning the ropes" about restoration and about working in a partnership, and for understanding more about business. As he TOOK STOCK of his resources for dealing with the partner disagreement, he realized that his *Situation* was excellent. He had decided to enter this partnership to see if he wanted to become a contractor and restorer. At the same time he had other pressures: he was in school, and he had a very low income. Despite these negatives, he appraised his *Situation* as good. His *Supports* were good. He had a live-in partner who would listen sympathetically as he recounted his aggravations and would actually help him at the property. In addition, his father knew a good deal about partnerships. In general, he felt pretty good about his *Self.*

But John's *Strategies* for coping with new situations were limited. He often whined and complained and acted as if he could not control things that happened to him. To TAKE CHARGE, he realized that he needed to increase his *Strategies.* To do this, he asked himself, "Should I change them, think about them differently, manage my reactions to stress, or take no action?'' John knew he needed to move from taking no action to taking action, learning to negotiate and assert himself. He actually TOOK CHARGE by suggesting that they dissolve the partnership. No one wanted that, so he started negotiations about different ways to work together that would be mutually beneficial. The problem is not resolved yet, but John feels as if he is doing something, not just complaining.

Let's return to the mid-life man quoted earlier who was depressed about having ''nowhere to go'' and see how he could TAKE CHARGE of his work transition. He felt that he was a fairly good coper, that he used lots of *Strategies,* and that he had good *Supports* at home. What he wanted to change was his *Situation.* He had several choices: talk with his boss and suggest a brainstorming session about how he could be more useful to the company; join a support group at his church called ''So you're having a mid-life crisis''; or seek career counseling and think systematically about what he really wanted to do with the rest of his life. If he did not want to take direct action, another possible approach would be to try to change the meaning of his work situation by telling himself that work is only one part of life and directly focusing more on strengthening his life outside work. He could also choose to manage his reactions to his work by relaxation or by putting everything on hold and doing nothing. In other words, he has lots of choices about how to take charge of his *Situation.*

To summarize: Most of us confront work transitions throughout most of our lives. Recognizing that work transitions are characterized by different needs as we move in, through, and out, we can apply the steps previously outlined in this book to master these changes. The key elements in achieving this mastery are APPROACHING CHANGE by understanding the transition process; TAKING STOCK of our resources for coping; and TAKING CHARGE by strengthening those resources.

8

Profiting from Change

R OSALYN and Jimmy Carter, who seemed to feel bitter and defeated after leaving the White House to return to Georgia in 1981, wrote a book about their experiences and toured the country with tales of how they grew from pain. Betty Ford turned her drug addiction into a mission to help others by founding the Betty Ford Center. Lee Iacocca, despite being fired by Ford Motor Company, became a folk hero by saving the Chrysler Corporation from extinction. All these people turned adversity into opportunity.

Stories such as these attract and intrigue all of us. Every disaster cannot be turned into an inspirational success, but every person can be helped to master change. Whether you are like Lisa (who moved to a new city for the "perfect" job and after a year is still depressed), like Mary (who is caught between an aging mother and two adult "children"), or any of the other people whose transitions are analyzed in this book, you can learn to cope creatively with change and to profit from it.

"Profiting from change" relates more to how you feel about your ability to handle, manage, or master transitions than to the specific job, house, or partner you have when the transition is over.

I don't want to imply that everyone can profit from every transition. Some are just too difficult. As one mother, whose two teenage children were drug users and constantly risking their lives, says, "This experience made me totally lose confidence in myself and my ability to be a parent." In other words, surviving a transition doesn't guarantee that one will also profit from it. But in talking with those who have negotiated their transitions successfully and profited from change, I identified several characteristic components of their success: increased *options,* informed *understanding,* and a feeling of *control.* One man reported having great feelings of hopelessness throughout two years in a job search. After that period, he concluded, "If I can weather that, I can weather anything. I will never be that upset again. In addition, I have more understanding of what one goes through after one loses a job and before one gets another one."

This trio—*options, understanding,* and *control*—does not *guarantee* a fairy-tale ending to a transition. Our profiting from change may not be as dramatic as Betty Ford's or Lee Iacocca's experience, but the subtle changes we feel may be as important to us as the dramatic ones. I believe that we have profited from change when we feel we have more options than we did before, when we have increased our understanding of the underlying and recurring issues that accompany any transition, and when we have increased our feeling that we can control and take charge of our lives.

Increasing Your Options

The concept of *options* includes elements of desire and hope that there is an alternative route. Seeing, creating, and using options are crucial to passing through life's transitions successfully. I have learned from my work that one of the factors most likely to transform a transition into a crisis is the inability to see the options, or choices, for escaping from a bad situation. Often men and women portrayed in crisis in the media are those who don't see any options.

We can search for options both in the external world and in our own internal world. Let's see how they differ and how we can identify them.

External options are opportunities that exist in a tangible sense: a job, a school, a person who will help you. For example, for residents of many rural areas, completing a college degree presents special obstacles. There may be no college at all in their town or only a two-year college that requires a long commute. For Ann, who lived in a small town and worked for the telephone company, the option of attending college was unavailable until the phone company and a university offered extension classes in her town for telephone employees. Ann explains her use of options this way. She had the dream of attending college, but because she lived in a rural community she had no access to a college. As soon as extension courses were available to her, she enrolled. She exercised choice when there was an external opportunity to do so.

Less tangible are the options that depend on your perceptions. When my colleague and I studied clerical workers, we asked, "Generally, in change situations how do you perceive options?" Ninety-four percent said that they saw more than one option. However, when asked, "For the transition you selected as one that really changed your life this past year, how many options did you perceive?" over 34 percent said they saw only one. These responses provided an important insight. People in the midst of a transition that is really altering their lives often freeze and can see only one option.[1]

In summary: Sometimes we do not exercise choices because there are no external or tangible opportunities, but at other times we just can't see the possibilities. One way to overcome this myopia is by TAKING STOCK, which will help you pinpoint which of your coping resources are low. Then you can begin TAKING CHARGE by generating new options for improving your *Situation, Self, Supports,* and *Strategies.*

This all sounds easy but we know that the process of generating and perceiving options can be difficult. How can we trigger it?

The triggering process is often not a conscious one. I can think of several examples of how it happened for other people, and maybe they will be instructive for you. Remember the story of the couple who had put their bed in the middle of the room? They were having serious psychological problems. They sought help from outsiders who noticed and commented on the unusual room arrangement, and this triggered a constructive brainstorming process that helped them identify options that they had not been able to see before.

In another case, a business executive named Mort was prompted unexpectedly into creating options for himself. After retiring from the business he founded, Mort found that his colleagues no longer sought his company for lunch. Miserable and depressed, he could see no way to overcome this negative side of retirement. Then Mort received a phone call from an executive with another company asking him to address participants in a preretirement seminar. This turned the tide. As he prepared the speech, Mort began to see new possibilities for his own life, helping employees and companies with the transition from work to retirement. He wrote a book on the subject and created a new life and career for himself, lecturing on the topic all over the country.

In the case of Brian, the inspiration for generating options was triggered by exposure to role models of other paraplegics.

These examples provide a lesson: There is no single magic way to get the ball rolling. For some people in transition, options suddenly become evident because they read something in a book or newspaper; they talk to a friend; they have a confrontation. The critical ingredient is remaining committed to the importance of the search and to "hang in there" for as long as it takes.

Informed Understanding

"If only I had known then what I know now."

How often have you said or heard this expression? I use it here because it sums up so well the importance of being able to predict, anticipate, and understand our life transitions. The need for predictability in life may explain the popularity of so-called stage theories that assign certain characteristics to each phase of our lives, implying that regardless of who you are, you are doomed to live through these chronological phases.

But in the absence of such certainty about the timing and types of transitions we will face, we must be satisfied with knowing that we will all experience both events and nonevents continually; and that by strengthening the ability to understand them and by exercising coping skills, we will be better prepared to master the transitions and not allow them to control us.

All of us have periods when everything seems to be going along fine: we work, play, love, and don't think too much about it. But then change may intrude in our lives and make us feel "out of sync." Suddenly we are taking a personal inventory, thinking about who we are and where we're going. We may face a crisis of confidence or competence.

Many report that when they go through transitions, they become self-centered. When they realize that it is perfectly normal to soul-search at times of transition, they express relief. I have learned to expect stock-taking and soul-searching whenever change occurs.

Although every transition is unique, one characteristic they all share is that they challenge our sense of who we are—our fundamental identity.

Although much of our sense of ourselves is established when we are young, we are constantly reassessing and redefining who we are. As we choose a particular job, educational institution, partner, or place of residence, we accept and incorporate some factors into our identity and rule out others.

This is true even for people who seem to be experiencing very disparate transitions, such as a high school football hero who has just moved to a new school and a business executive who has just retired. Both are asking themselves who they are now that their established roles and identities have disappeared. Will they try to continue to define themselves as before, or will they be able to incorporate new dimensions to their identity?

The comparison of the football hero and the retired business executive helps demonstrate that certain themes surface over and over again as people in transition sort out what to do next.

But our identity is not made up solely of external factors such as the job we hold or where we live. It is also composed of psychological factors, and these, too, are affected anytime we are in transition.

I have found that simply identifying some of these common themes and giving them names, such as *belonging* and *mattering*, can be helpful both in understanding why a transition causes discomfort and in moving on to develop strategies for coping with that discomfort.

Here is a list of some of the most common themes that have surfaced as I have worked with people in transition:

Belonging. Do you feel a part of things, or do you feel marginal? Getting divorced, caring for an aging parent, and becoming the boss of a group of employees are examples of role changes. The process of moving from one role to another takes time and may generate feelings that you don't quite "belong" yet. It helps to know that marginality is often temporary and that rituals can help you slip into your new role. Knowing that the feeling of being on the edge and peripheral is temporary can help engender the control you need to master change.

Mattering. Transitions can make you wonder whether you make a difference, whether others miss you, still depend upon you, and care about you. Sociologist Morris Rosenberg has labeled this phenomenon as *mattering*—the feeling of being wanted, needed, missed, depended upon, or the object of attention by others. He and his colleagues found that mattering is such a powerful motive that it can even deter delinquent behavior among adolescents. Adolescents who feel they matter to someone else are less likely to engage in delinquent acts.[2] We have seen many people—such as Mort, the business executive—for whom retiring from work evoked feelings of not mattering. Although most of the literature on mattering points to it as positive, there is another, more stressful side to mattering when we feel that too many people are dependent on us.

As our roles change, sometimes we feel we matter too little; at other times we feel we matter too much. The knowledge that mattering matters all through life and that it will be played out very differently as our life circumstances change can soften some of the anxieties that might crop up.

Competence. Transitions often require that you learn a new skill. How often have you heard people in transition claim that they are unable to cope with the complex demands of the new job, of being a stepparent, or moving with young children to a new community?

The feelings of incompetence often evoked by new roles can be the first step toward gaining competence, as transitions become triggers for learning.

Intimacy. Close interpersonal relationships with a range of people—spouse, lover, parents, children, friends—can offer strong support in times of stress, as well as warmth and color to your existence. The form of intimacy is less important than the fact that it exists throughout your life. In order to be happy and to function well, we all need the affect, affirmation, and feedback that intimacy provides; and when an intimate relationship is lost—through death, divorce, or a change in commitment—the crucial issue is whether you can "reinvest" and replace it.

Renewal. Stagnation and renewal are two sides of a coin. Stagnation represents a kind of death in life: a feeling of boredom, of being boxed in, a lack of commitment to anything. For example, people working dead-end jobs may be stagnating. Renewal can occur if these workers balance the stagnation with positive activities like changing jobs, or seeing the job in a different way, or focusing their energy and commitment on other aspects of their lives. At its best, the concept of renewal implies taking care of oneself and the possibility of helping others so that they can continue making contributions.

 To summarize: I have found that people in transition profit from change when they understand what is happening to them, especially the way they see themselves. With each transition they once again face shifts in their identities, the way they define themselves. In addition, they are confronted with questions: Do I matter? Do I belong? Am I competent to deal with this? Will the transition affect my needs for intimacy? Will the transition help me meet my need for renewal?

Feeling in Control

The ability to influence events, things, persons, and themselves gives people a sense of control. Recent experiments provide evidence that when people are given some measure of control over their work, they invest more of themselves in it and their productivity increases.[3]

Judith Rodin, a psychologist, studied the importance of feeling in control for residents of a nursing home. In one experiment, she compared residents who were given some elements of control over their environment with others who were not. Daniel Goleman, psychologist and *New York Times* science reporter, describes some of her findings. In one study of elderly men and women living in convalescent homes, those given control over aspects of their lives lived longer than those given no control.[4]

Another perspective on the issue of feeling in control emerged from an interview I conducted with wives of pro football players. As the wife of a football hero said, "It just doesn't seem fair. For years I have been on hold while he has become a national hero. When will it be my turn? I feel as if my life is controlled by his schedule and needs, not mine."

Another wife felt that both adults in a marriage or partnership should have equal control over who cooks, cleans, mends, and takes children to doctors and dentists; over who moves for a better job; over whose life "counts." She wondered, "Will that kind of equality ever exist for me?"

Divorce is another example of a situation in which we may have—or perceive that we have—more or less control than others who are affected. If I were to interview the cast of characters involved in a particular divorce, I would find as many different stories as there are individuals. The couple's children, for example, might wish to prevent the divorce but realize that they are powerless to do so. The parents of the divorcing couple might also feel that they lack control. The couple who made the decision to divorce may feel in control of the decision, or one member of the couple may feel that it has been imposed on him or her.

In divorce as in any other transition, people may use different methods to cope with the problem of feeling out of control. They may try to change the situation by negotiating, receiving mediation, cajoling, or even by legal means such as promoting legislation to protect grandparents' rights. Others might try to change the perceived meaning of divorce with comments like, "This will really be better for the kids." Still others try to relax in the face of a difficult situation by jogging, meditating, or relaxing.

Thus, individuals have two kinds of control—the degree to which they influence their life circumstances and the degree to which they control how they cope with and handle life circumstances. I used to say to my teenage son, "I cannot change the single-minded coach who expects you to play even with a concussion, but I can help you learn how to cope more effectively by suggesting that you change the situation by getting off the football team; that you change the meaning of the situation by beginning to see football as just one activity and the coach's put-down of you whenever you don't score as irrelevant; or that you cope by trying to relax, breathe deeply, and imagine yourself as you want to be on the field."

As our lives ebb and flow, it is inevitable that sometimes we feel we are in control of external events and at other times we do not. The challenge is to know and to understand that we will have feelings of lack of control and that we can do something about them.

A Final Word

In the study of men whose jobs were eliminated, my colleagues and I found that most of them felt "hit on the head" and "kicked in the back" when they first learned of the RIF. They were terrified of the change, yet six months later typical reports from these men were "I feel like a king" and "I now know I can handle anything." They had been challenged by change.

One young woman's story is illustrative of the possibilities that can grow even from an unwanted change. She explains:

I wanted to attend a small liberal arts college out of state. I was accepted, enrolled, and received some scholarship aid. But the cost of traveling and living on a campus away from home was expensive, and as my sophomore year was ending, my parents said that they could not afford to keep me there any longer.

Faced with returning to my home state, where I could cut my

educational costs by qualifying for in-state tuition and living at home, I was upset at leaving the campus and my new friends, but I saw no alternative to doing so.

The transition was difficult—adjusting to a huge, anonymous institution, getting bad advice about what courses to take. But one thing I knew was that at my previous institution, where I was a top editor on the small campus newspaper, I'd pretty much gained all the practical experience I could in my chosen career of journalism. So as soon as I enrolled in the state university, I marched into the office of the daily campus newspaper, volunteered to work, and within a few weeks had (a) a whole group of new, interesting friends, and (b) prospects for an exciting new professional challenge, and (c) exposure to all sorts of advantages of being on a large campus in a big city.

The young woman who wrote this profited from change because she learned to master a transition—even one she did not want.

I wrote about Brian in chapter 5. His case is so inspirational that I want to update his story here. As we saw, over time Brian was able to turn his tragedy into a challenge. At the moment he is in a graduate program with a very supportive adviser and plans to marry someone he met in graduate school.

How did he manage to do all this after his devastating tragic accident? Clearly, Brian's number-one resource is his resilient personality. The constancy of his extremely supportive mother was also crucial to his turnaround. In addition, the supportive adviser and the meaningful relationship all contributed. I asked his mother what had been the most help to Brian, and she said that probably of equal importance to his own personality was the inspiration of other paraplegics who were living rewarding lives. His physical therapist, for example, competes in wheelchair racing. Seeing the example of a paraplegic who could succeed professionally and in athletics inspired Brian to join the Wheelchair Association of America. Now Brian keeps himself in excellent condition and participates in wheelchair marathons. Another role model for Brian was the wheelchair salesman, also a paraplegic, who showed him that mobility was possible, instructed him in how to use the wheelchair, and even inspired Brian to learn to drive.

Brian had the good fortune of being a resilient person with tremendous supports. But there was more. He had a choice: to fold up his tent and die, or to fight with all his energy for life. Once he realized that he wanted to live, he began to focus seriously on how to live with his disability. The process of "getting it together" was a slow one; it took about five years. If you had spoken to Brian one year after his accident, the story would have been different.

As I pointed out when describing the transition process, reactions to a transition change over time. At one point, a transition might seem "for worse" and at another point "for better." To judge whether you have profited from change you have to ask yourself: Do you see options you did not see before? Have you been able to develop new roles, relationships, routines, and assumptions that have meaning and that are comfortable for you? Clearly, Brian could answer yes to these questions.

Life for most people really is a series of ups and downs. We know that one can be as overwhelmed with a sought-after life change as with a dreaded one. What is needed is what this book is all about: a series of actions to take, thoughts to think, and decisions to make.

Overwhelmed suggests strategies for coping with life's ups and downs. By looking at your resources for coping—your four S's—in a sensible, rational way, you need no longer be overwhelmed. In fact you are TAKING CHARGE of your life. A marathoner's decision to enter a training program may be as important as the actual training. Like the marathoner, it is up to you to decide whether to step up to the starting line. When you do so, you'll realize that you're already halfway to the finish.

Notes

1. The Transition Process

1. B.L. Neugarten, "Time, Age, and the Life Cycle," *American Journal of Psychiatry* 136 (1979): 887–94.
2. L.I. Pearlin and M.A. Lieberman, "Social Sources of Emotional Distress," in *Research in Community and Mental Health,* ed. R. Simmons (Greenwich, Conn.: JAI Press, 1979).
3. N.K. Schlossberg and Z.B. Leibowitz, "Organizational Support Systems as Buffers to Job Loss," *Journal of Vocational Behavior* 18 (1980): 204–7.

2. Transitions: Their Infinite Variety

1. J.M. Chiappone, "Infertility as a Nonevent: Impact, Coping, and Differences Between Men and Women" (Ph.D. diss., University of Maryland, 1984).
2. G.O. Hagestad, "The Social Meanings of Age," in *The Adult Years: Continuity and Change,* ed. N.K. Schlossberg et al. (Owings Mills, Md.: International University Consortium, 1985).

3. TAKING STOCK of your *Situation*

1. C. Peterson and M.E.P. Seligman, "Causal Explanations as a Risk Factor for Depression: Theory and Evidence," *Psychological Review* 91 (1984): 347–74.
2. R.S. Lazarus and S. Folkman. *Stress, Appraisal, and Coping* (New York: Springer, 1984).
3. M.K. McEwen, S.R. Komives, and N.K. Schlossberg, *Departing the College Presidency: Voices of Women and Men in Transition* (College Park, Md.: University of Maryland, 1988). Research in progress.

4. N.K. Schlossberg and Z.B. Leibowitz, "Organizational Support Systems as Buffers to Job Loss," *Journal of Vocational Behavior* 18 (1980): 204–17.

5. R. Seidenberg, *Corporate Wives: Corporate Casualties* (New York: Am Com Division of American Management Association, 1973).

4. TAKING STOCK of Your *Self* and *Supports*

1. W. Schain, conversation with author about Sandra Levy's research. Washington, D.C., July 1981.

2. G. Baruch, R. Barnett, and C. Rivers, *Lifeprints: New Patterns of Love and Work for Today's Women* (New York: New American Library, 1983).

3. C. Peterson and M.E.P. Seligman, "Causal Explanations as a Risk Factor for Depression: Theory and Evidence," *Psychological Review* 91(3) (1984): 347–74.

4. R.J. Trotter, "Stop Blaming Yourself," *Psychology Today,* Feb. 1987, 31–9 (report of Seligman's work).

5. D. Kiersey, and M. Bates, *Please Understand Me: Character and Temperament Types* (Del Mar, Calif.: Prometheus Nemesis Book Company, 1984).

6. R.S. Lazarus and S. Folkman, *Stress, Appraisal, and Coping* (New York: Springer, 1984), p. 19.

7. M.F. Lowenthal and D. Chiriboga, "Responses to Stress" in *Four Stages of Life: A Comparative Study of Men and Women Facing Transitions,* ed. M.F. Lowenthal, M. Thurnher, and D. Chiriboga (San Francisco: Jossey-Bass, 1975).

8. G. Caplan, "The Family as Support System," in *Support Systems and Mutual Help: Multidisciplinary Exploration,* ed. G. Caplan and M. Killilea (New York: Grune and Stratton, 1976).

9. R.L. Kahn and T.C. Antonucci, "Convoys Over the Life Course: Attachment, Roles, and Social Support," in *Lifespan Development and Behavior,* vol. 3, ed. P.B. Baltes and O.G. Brim, Jr. (New York: Academic Press, 1980).

10. G.O. Hagestad, "Vertical Bonds: Intergenerational Relationships," in *The Adult Years: Continuity and Change,* ed. N.K. Schlossberg et al. (Owings Mills, Md.: International University Consortium, 1985).

11. L.B. Rubin, *Just Friends: The Role of Friendship in our Lives* (New York: Harper & Row, 1985).

12. S.K. Pollack, "Grieving and Growing," *Journal of Counseling and Development* 67 (October 1988): 117.

13. Hagestad, "Vertical Bonds," 133–66.

14. Kahn and Antonucci, "Convoys Over the Life Course," 273.

5. TAKING STOCK of Your *Strategies*

1. L.I. Pearlin and C. Schooler, "The Structure of Coping," *Journal of Health and Social Behavior,* 19 (1978): 2–21.
2. R.S. Lazarus and S. Folkman, *Stress, Appraisal, and Coping* (New York: Springer, 1984).
3. G.I. Nierenberg, *Fundamentals of Negotiating* (New York: Hawthorn Books, 1973).
4. L. Caine, *Widow* (New York: William Morrow, 1974).
5. B.L. Neugarten, "Time, Age, and the Life Cycle," *American Journal of Psychiatry* 136 (1979): 887–94.
6. "Rites and Independence: New Ceremonies for New People," *Ms.,* November 1984.
7. B. Myerhoff, Film, "Rites of Renewal" (Owings Mills, Md: International University Consortium and Ohio University, 1985); "Rites and Signs of Ripening and Intertwining of Ritual, Time and Growing Older," in *Age and Anthropological Theory,* ed. D. Kertzer and J. Keitch (Ithaca: Cornell University Press, 1984).
8. S.E. Taylor, "Adjustment to Threatening Events: A Theory of Cognitive Adaptation," quoted in *APA News Release,* 1 December 1983.
9. G.E. Vaillant, *Adaptation to Life* (Boston: Little, Brown, 1977).
10. C. Wade, "Humor," in *Every Woman's Emotional Well-Being,* ed. C. Tavris (New York: Doubleday, 1986).
11. H.H. Santmyer, . . . *And Ladies of the Club* (New York: G.P. Putnam & Sons, 1986).
12. S.K. Pollack, "Grieving and Growing," *Journal of Counseling and Development* 67 (October 1988): 117.

6. Your Action Plan for Mastering Change

1. J. Viorst, *Necessary Losses* (New York: Simon & Schuster, 1986).

7. TAKING CHARGE of Your Work Transitions

1. M.R. Louis, "Surprise and Sense Making: What Newcomers Experience in Entering Unfamiliar Organizational Settings," *Administrative Science Quarterly* 25 (June 1980).
2. C. Hyatt and L. Gottlieb, *When Smart People Fail* (New York: Simon & Schuster, 1987).
3. J. Bardwick, *Plateauing* (New York: AMACOM, 1986).
4. Louis, "Surprise and Sense Making," 74.
5. P. Marris, *Loss and Change* (New York: Pantheon Books, 1974).

8. Profiting from Change

1. I. Charner and N.K. Schlossberg, "Variations by Theme: The Life Transitions of Clerical Workers," *Vocational Guidance Quarterly* 34 (1986): 212–24.
2. M. Rosenberg and B.C. McCullough, "Mattering: Inferred Significance to Parents and Mental Health Among Adolescents," in *Research in Community and Mental Health,* vol. 2, ed. R. Simmons (Greenwich, Conn.: JAI Press, 1981).
3. R.E. Walton, *Innovating to Compete: Lessons for Diffusing and Managing Change in the Workplace* (San Francisco: Jossey-Bass, 1987).
4. D. Goleman, "Feeling of Control Viewed as Central in Mental Health," *New York Times,* October 7, 1986, C1 and C11.

Index

About the Author

NANCY K. SCHLOSSBERG, a professor in the Department of Counseling and Personnel Services, University of Maryland, College Park, speaks and writes about mid-life, adults in transition, and higher education. She has been honored for her work by the American Psychological Association, the National Career Development Association, the American College Personnel Association and the National Association of Student Personnel Administrators.